✍

Ten men departed from Oakland and rode on horseback to Yosemite, up to the Tuolumne Meadows, down to Mono Lake, to Tahoe and back to Sacramento, where the weary climbers embarked on a boat for Oakland. It was rough adventure, killing rattlesnakes and foraging for food—compensated by the majestic eloquence of the mountains around them. Awakening in transparent golden sunlight, they put in strenuous days and when day ended, made their beds in aromatic spruce.

It was 1870 and the men were the University of California Excursion Party.

They were early ecologists, disturbed by what they found—deserted mine towns and streams muddied by placer mining. Their knowledgeable concern 100 years ago spurred action to retain the beauty of the High Sierras as it is today. This is the story of an adventure in 1870. But it is still a definitive, enriching guide for the twentieth century traveller who wants to deepen his experience of this majestic portion of Earth.

A Journal of
RAMBLINGS
through the
HIGH SIERRA
of California

by the University Excursion Party

Joseph LeConte

A SIERRA CLUB / BALLANTINE BOOK
An Intext Publisher
New York

Library of Congress Catalog Card Number: 60-16805

SBN 345-02264-5-125

This edition published by arrangement with Sierra Club Books.

First Printing: May, 1971

Cover art by Norman Adams

Printed in the United States of America

SIERRA CLUB
1050 Mills Tower, San Francisco, California 94104
250 West 57th Street, New York, N.Y. 10019

BALLANTINE BOOKS, INC.
101 Fifth Avenue, New York, N.Y. 10003

CONTENTS

FOREWORD

Joseph LeConte came to California in 1869 to
take part in the organization of the new University of California which had grown out of the
small college at Oakland. Professor LeConte at
once entered upon his duties as professor of natural sciences and very soon his profound scholarship and his talent for teaching made themselves
felt both in the University itself and in the surrounding community. As years went by he came
to embody the very ideal of a college professor
and his students felt for him an affection sur-
passed only by their admiration for his scholarship.

Joseph LeConte was a native of Georgia, born
at "Woodmanston," in Liberty County, Febru-
ary 26, 1823. He received the degrees of Bach-
elor of Arts and Master of Arts at the University
of Georgia, and the degree of Doctor of Medi-
cine at the College of Physicians and Surgeons,
New York. For a brief period he practiced medi-
cine at Macon, Georgia, but his tastes were more

towards scientific study, and in 1850 he went to
Harvard to study with Agassiz. The character of
this great teacher undoubtedly had a strong influence upon LeConte's life. "To explain how
much I owe to him," he writes in his Autobiography, "it is only necessary to say that for fifteen
months I was associated with him in the most
intimate personal way, from eight to ten hours
a day, and every day, usually including Sun-
days." With this rich experience and this train-
ing in scholarship behind him, he began his
career as a teacher. At Oglethorpe University,
Georgia, and then at the University of Georgia,
he taught not only the natural sciences, including
mechanics, physics, chemistry, geology, and
botany, but also natural theology and French.
In 1857 he was appointed professor of chemistry
and geology in South Carolina College, where he
remained during the Civil War. In his Autobiography Professor LeConte describes some of the
adventures and hardships of this period. During
the gloomy days of the Reconstruction, he and
his brother, John, learned of the proposed University of California and applied for the pro-
fessorships to which they were promptly elected.

It was with this background that Joseph Le
Conte, now forty-six years of age, entered upon
an entirely new period of life. "These early years
in California," he writes, "were very active ones
for me, the wonderful new country, so different
from any that I had previously seen, the climate,
the splendid scenery, the active, energetic people,
and the magnificent field for scientific, and espe-

cially for geological investigations, stimulating my intellectual activity to the highest degree." This sense of a new era in his life and his enthusiasm for its activities are everywhere apparent in the Journal of Ramblings, *in which he records the experiences of his first excursion into the mountain regions of the Pacific Coast. "J never enjoyed anything else so much in my life,"* he writes in the Autobiography, *"—perfect health, the merry party of young men, the glorious scenery, and, above all, the magnificent opportunity for studying mountain origin and structure. Observations made on this and later trips formed the basis for ten or eleven papers on this most fundamental and fascinating subject and on others closely related. J subsequently made many similar trips, but this remained the most delightful, because, as it was the first, everything was so new to me and so different from anything that J had previously experienced."*

For thirty-two years Professor LeConte taught at the University of California, constantly enriching his life with new experiences and passing on that enrichment to succeeding classes of students. Meanwhile his scientific papers grew into volumes, some of which are still in constant use. Notable among them are Elements of Geology, *which has appeared in a number of editions,* Religion and Science, *and* Evolution and Its Relation to Religious Thought. *During the last year of his life he began his autobiography, a work that was completed and edited after his death by Professor William Dallam Armes.*

The last days of Joseph LeConte were spent most happily in Yosemite Valley. Following the wedding of his son, Joseph N. LeConte, at Berkeley, in June, 1901, he visited the valley with his daughter. He planned to join the Sierra Club in its first large outing party in the Sierra, and for two days he enjoyed to the utmost the delights of companionship in the midst of the beloved scenes. His strength failed, however, and with but a day's illness he passed quietly away. The story of these last hours is touchingly told by Professor Frank Soulé in the Sierra Club Bulletin and by Professor Armes in the preface to the Autobiography.

The name of Joseph LeConte is associated almost as closely with the Yosemite and the High Sierra as it is with the University of California. Following his first visit with "The University Excursion Party" in 1870, he made a number of trips to Yosemite, Tuolumne Meadows, and Lake Tahoe. In 1872, and again in 1875, he studied the glacial system of the Tuolumne and corroborated John Muir's statement that there were living glaciers in the Sierra Nevada. In 1889 he was delighted to revisit the scenes of the 1870 trip with another party of his pupils, this time accompanied by his son, Joseph N. LeConte, of whom he later wrote in the Autobiography: "He has since become the best camper and mountaineer I ever knew, tramping four or five hundred miles in the Sierra every summer and probably knowing them better than any other living man, unless possibly Mr. John Muir." Professor LeConte was one of the charter members of the Sierra Club, founded in 1892, but his absence in Europe during the period of organization prevented his taking an active part in the initial steps.

The memory of Joseph LeConte is such a rich heritage that it should be familiar to all who love the Sierra, especially to members of the Sierra Club. In the early days of the club many of its members were students or associates of "Professor Joe" and rejoiced in knowing him and in hearing his lectures. New generations, however, must depend upon the printed page, and it is for this reason that the Sierra Club now reprints this Journal of Ramblings. The original edition, issued in 1875, was distributed among the members of the party and their friends. It has long been extremely scarce and is to be found in but few libraries. In 1900 the Journal was reprinted in the Sierra Club Bulletin, and a small number of copies was issued in separate form. This second edition is now quite as scarce as the first, with the result that this delightful narrative has been hidden from a great many persons who would enjoy it.

In publishing the present edition an effort has been made to retain as much of the character of the original book as possible without attempting in any way to make a facsimile. The text of the edition of 1900 departed from that of 1875 in a few instances for the purpose of correcting slight errors and of conforming to more recent terminology. There were also a few trivial omissions. Most of these deviations have been followed in the present edition and a few others of a similar nature have been added.

To this point the Foreword is the same as that written for the 1930 edition. A comment on the present edition is added. There are no changes in the text except that the bibliographical notes at the end have been brought to date.

FRANCIS P. FARQUHAR

Berkeley, California,
August 10, 1960

PREFACE

About the first week before the end of the First Session of the University of California, several young men, students of the University, invited me to join them in a camping party for the Yosemite and the High Sierra. The party was to go in regular pioneer style, cooking their own provisions, and sleeping under the open sky whenever a convenient place was found; each man was to bestride his own horse, carry his own bedding behind his saddle, and his clothing, with the exception of one change of underwear, on his back. This was, it is true, a little rougher and harder than anything I had ever undertaken; but still I was fond of adventure, and longed to enjoy the glories of Yosemite and the beauties of the Sierra, and, more than all, to study mountain structure and mountain sculpture, as exhibited there on a magnificient scale. I therefore at once accepted the offer. The party was forthwith organized, ten in number. Mr. Hawkins, who understood something of mountain life, was commissioned to buy the necessary supplies and the general outfit, such as camp utensils, pack-horse and pack-saddle, and have all in readiness that we might start the very first day after commencement.

To while away my idle moments in camp, and to preserve some *souvenir* of the party, of the incidents, and of the scenery, I jotted down, from time to time, these wayside notes.

J. L'C.

Joseph LeConte
A JOURNAL OF RAMBLINGS
THROUGH THE HIGH SIERRA
OF CALIFORNIA
1870

A Journal of Ramblings Through The High Sierra of California

JULY 21, 1870.—Amid many kind and cheering words, mingled with tender regrets; many encouragements, mingled with earnest entreaties to take care of myself, and to keep out of *drafts* and *damp* while sleeping on the *bare ground* in the *open air*, many half-suppressed tears, concealed beneath bright smiles, I left my home and dear ones this morning. Surely I must have a heroic and dangerous air about me, for my little baby boy shrinks from my rough flannel shirt and broad-brim hat, as did the baby son of Hector from *his* brazen corslet and beamy helm and nodding plume. I snatch a kiss and hurry away to our place of rendezvous.

After much bustle, confusion, and noisy preparation, saddling, cinching, strapping blanket rolls, packing camp utensils and provisions, we are fairly ready at 10 A.M. Saluted by cheers from manly throats, and handkerchief-waving by the white hands of women, we leave Oakland at a sweeping trot, Hawkins leading the pack; while the long handle of our frying-pan, sticking straight up through a hole in the bag, and the merry jingling of *tin* pans, *tin* cups and coffee pot—"tintinnabulation"—proclaimed the nature of our mission.

We are in high spirits; although I confess to some misgivings when I heard from the Captain that we would ride thirty miles today, for I have not been on horseback for ten years. But I am determined not to be an incumbrance to the merry party. We started from Oakland seven in number. One will join us tonight in Livermore Valley. Two others, having gone to Stockton to procure horses, will join us at Graysonville. Without any remarkable incident we rode along the level plain which borders the bay about fifteen miles, and reached our lunch-ground near Hayward, at 1 P.M. Here we fed our horses and rested two hours.

Started again at 3 P.M. Our ride took us over the Contra Costa Ridge, by Hayward Pass, into Amador and Livermore valleys, and then along these valleys, the noble outline of Mt. Diablo looming finely in the distance on our left. I observe everything narrowly, for all is new to me, and so different from anything in the Eastern states. Livermore Valley is an extensive, rich, level plain, separating the Contra Costa from the Mt. Diablo Ridge. It is surround by mountains on every side, and the scenery is really fine. Much pleased to find the mountains, on their northern and eastern slopes, so green and well wooded. I have been accustomed to see them from Oakland only on their southern and western slopes, which are almost treeless, and, at this season, brown and sere. Much interested in watching the habits of burrowing squirrels and burrowing owls, especially the amicable manner in which they live together in the same burrows.

After riding about ten miles, we arrived, a little before sunset, at Dublin, a little village of a few houses. Here we found tolerable camping-ground, and ought to have stopped for the night; but, against my advice, the party, buoyant and thoughtless, concluded to go on to Laddsville,* where one of the party would join us, and had promised to prepare forage for our horses and camp for ourselves. It was a foolish mistake. From this time our ride was very tedious and fatiguing. The miles seemed to stretch out before us longer and longer. The hiliarious and somewhat noisy spirits of the young men gradually died away. After some abortive attempts at a song, some miserable failures in the way of jokes, we pursued our weary way in silence. Night closed upon us while we were still many miles from Laddsville. Lights ahead! Are these Laddsville? We hope so. Onward we press; but the

* This place is now called Livermore.

lights seem to recede from us. Still onward, seemingly three or four miles; but no nearer the lights. Are these *ignes fatui* sent to delude us. But courage! here comes someone.

"How far to Laddsville?"

"Three miles."

Onward we pressed, at least three miles. Again a wayfarer.

"How far to Laddsville?"

"Three and a half miles."

Again three or four miles onward; three or four miles of aching ankles and knees and hips and back, but no complaint.

"How many miles to Laddsville?"

"Five."

Again three or four miles of aching knees and hips and back. Wayfarers are becoming more numerous.

"How far to Laddsville?"

"Two miles."

"How far to Laddsville?"

"A little over a mile."

"How far to Laddsville?"—"How far to Laddsville?"—"To Laddsville?"

Ah! here it is at last. Yes, at last, about 10 P.M. that now celebrated place was actually reached; but too late for good camping. The companion who was to join us here was nowhere to be found. We hastily made arrangements for our horses in a neighboring stable, and camped on the bare, dusty ground, in an open space on the outskirts of the town. A good campfire and a hearty meal comforted us somewhat.

About 11:30 P.M. rolled ourselves in our blankets and composed ourselves for sleep. To our wearied spirits, we seem to have traveled at least fifty miles today. From the most accurate information we can get, however, the actual distance is only about thirty-five miles. Very foolish to go so far the first day.

JULY 22.—Estimating the whole mammalian population of Laddsville at two hundred, I am sure at least one hundred and fifty must be dogs. These kept up such an incessant barking all night, around us and at us, as we lay upon the ground, that we got little sleep. Near daybreak I sank into a deeper, sweeter sleep, when whoo! —oo-oo-oo!—whoo!!! the scream of a railroad train, passing within fifty feet, startled the night air and us. It is not surprising, then, that we got up reluctantly, and rather late, and very stiff and sore. Our breakfast, which consisted this morning of *fried bacon, cheese, cold bread,* and *good tea,* refreshed and comforted us greatly. While eating our breakfast, whoop! whoop! hurrah! our expected companion, Dell Linderman, came galloping in, with gun slung on shoulder. He did his best, by whip and spur and noise, to make a dashing entry, but his heavy, sluggish mare did not in the least sympathize with his enthusiasm. He had been looking for us the evening before, but had given us up, and went back to a friend's house, a little out of Laddsville.

Soon after sunrise, all the inhabitants of Laddsville, including, of course, the one hundred and fifty dogs, came crowding around us—the men to find out who we were, and where bound; the dogs to find out what it was they had been barking at all night. After we had severally satisfied these, our fellow creatures, both biped and quadruped—our fellow men and Darwinian cousins—we saddled and packed up, determined to profit by the experience of yesterday, and not to go more than twenty miles today. Our horses as well as ourselves have suffered from the travel of yesterday. We started late, about 8 A.M., proceeded only five miles, and stopped, 10 A.M., under the shade of a clump of oaks, near a mill. The air is still this morning, and the sun insufferably hot.

We here took cold lunch, and rested until 1 P.M. A cool breeze now springing up, we started, passed over the summit of Corral Hollow Pass and down by a very steep grade, I think about fifteen hundred feet in a mile, into "Corral Hollow," a very narrow cañon with only fifty to sixty yards width at the bottom, with high rocky cliffs on eitherside, which cuts through Mt. Diablo Range to the base. The road now ran in this cañon along a dry stream-bed for many miles, until it finally emerges on the San Joaquin plains.

In Amador and Livermore valleys, I observed the soil was composed of a drift of rounded pebbles, in stiff adobe clay—local drift from the mountains. In Corral Hollow the soil consists of pebbles and coarse sand, evidently river deposit. Fine sections showing cross lamination were observed. Mountains very steep on each side the gorge. Perpendicular cliffs of sandstone and limestone exposed in many places, sometimes worn into fantastic shapes, and often into caves. These caves, I hear, were once the haunts of robbers. Near the bottom of the gorge the irregularly stratified river sands are seen lying unconformably on the sandstone. We passed on our way some coal mines, which are now worked. These strata are probably cretaceous, belonging to the same horizon as the Mt. Diablo coal.

We rode ten or twelve miles down Corral Hollow, or about fifteen miles, this afternoon, and camped, 7 P.M., at a teamsters' camp, the permanent camp of the teamsters of the coalmine. From these men we bought feed for our horses; then cooked supper, and went to bed as early as possible.

JULY 23.—The whole party woke up this morning in good spirits, much refreshed by our supper and sleep last night. We got up at 4 A.M., cooked our breakfast, and were off by 5:30. At first we really enjoyed our ride in the cool morning air. In about an hour we emerged from Corral Hollow on the San Joaquin plains. There is still a fine cool breeze. "Why, this is delightful; the San Joaquin plains have been much slandered," thought we. As we advanced, however, we changed our opinion. Insufficiency of rain last winter has produced utter failure of crops. As far as the eye can reach, in every direction, only a bare desert plain is seen. The heat now became intense; the wind, though strong, was dry and burning. Over the perfectly level, dry, parched, dusty, and now desert plains, with baked lips and bleeding noses, we pressed on toward Grayson, where we expected to noon. "Grayson is on the San Joaquin River. It can't be far off, for yonder is water." Yes, surely yonder is water; do you not see its glistening surface?—its rolling billows running in the direction of the wind?—the reflection of the trees, which grow on the *farther* bank? Those white objects scattered over the glistening surface, with their images beneath: are these not sails on the river? Alas, no! It is all mirage. There is no water visible at all. The trees are trees which skirt the *nearer* bank of the river; the white objects are cottages on the desert plains. We could hardly believe it until we were deceived and undeceived half a dozen times. Parched with heat and thirst, and blinded with dust, we could easily appreciate the tantalizing effect of similar phenomena on the thirsty travelers of Sahara.

Onward, still onward, with parched throats, baked lips, and bleeding noses, we press. But even with parched throat, baked lips, and bleeding nose, one may enjoy the ludicrous, and even shake his gaunt sides with laughter; at least I found it so this morning. The circumstances were these: Hawkins early this morning killed a rabbit. Phelps, conceiving the idea that it would relish well, broiled on the glowing coals of our camp-fire tonight, offered to carry it. He did so for some time; but his frisky, foolish, unsteady filly, not liking the dangling rabbit, became restive, and the rabbit was dropped in disgust and left on the road. Stone, good-natured fellow, in simple kindness of heart, and also having the delights of broiled rabbit present in his imagination—the *picture* of broiled rabbit before his *mind's eye*, and the *fragrance* of broiled rabbit in his *mind's nose*—dismounted and picked it up. But essaying to mount his cowlike beast again, just when he had, with painful effort, climber up to his "saddle's eaves," and was about to heave his long dexter leg over and wriggle himself into his seat, the beast aforesaid, who had been attentively viewing the operation out of the external corner of his left eye started suddenly forward, and Stone, to his great astonishment, found himself on *his own* instead of his horse's back. Then commenced a wild careering over the dusty plain, with the saddle under his belly; a mad plunging and kicking, a general chasing by the whole party, including Stone himself, on foot; a laughing and shouting by all except Stone, until cinch and straps gave way, and saddle, blanket-roll, and clothing lay strewed upon the ground.

We had hardly picked up Stone's traps and mended his cinch and started on our way—the agitation of our diaphragms and the aching of our sides had hardly subsided—when Pomroy, sitting high-enthroned on his aged, misshapen beast, thinking to show the ease and grace of his perfect horsemanship, and also secretly desiring to ease the exquisite tenderness of his sitting-bones, quietly detached his right foot from the stirrup and swung it gracefully over the pommel, to sit a while in woman-fashion. But as soon as the shadow of his great top-boots fell across the eyes of "Old 67," that venerable beast, whether in the innocency of coltlike playfulness or a natural malignancy, made frantic by excessive heat and dust, began to kick and plunge and buck, until finally, by a sudden and dexterous arching of his back and a throwing down of his head, Pomroy was shot from the saddle like an arrow from a bow or a shell from a mortar; and sailing through mid-air with arms and legs widely extended, like the bird of Jove, descended in graceful parabolic curve and fell into the arms of his fond mother earth. Unwilling to encounter the wrath of his master, "Old 67" turned quickly and fled, with his mouth wide open, and his teeth all showing, as if enjoying a huge horse-laugh. Then commenced again the wild careering on the hot plains, the mad plunging and kicking, the shouting and laughing and chasing. The horse at last secured, Pomroy took him firmly by the bit, delivered one blow of his clenched fist upon his nose, and then gazed at him steadily with countenance full of solemn warning. In return, a wicked, unrepentant, vengeful gleam shot from the corner of the deep-sunk eye of "Old 67."

Onward, still onward, over the absolutely treeless and plantless desert, we rode for fifteen or more miles and reached Grayson about 12 M. Here we nooned and rested until 4 P.M. Two of our party, viz.: Cobb and Bolton, joined up here from Stockton, where they had gone to procure horses. While resting here, we took a delightful swim in the San Joaquin River. Delightfully refreshing while in the water; but on coming out the wind felt as hot and dry and fiery as if it blew out of a furnace. Caught a few fish here, and enjoyed them for lunch. Bought some peaches, and devoured them with a kind of ravenous fierceness. Ah! how delicious in this parched country!

Grayson is a small, insignificant village, with a half-dozen or more buildings, among which there are, of course, the hotel and the post-office. I took advantage of the latter to send off a letter to my wife—a very short letter—assuring her of my health, and that I was doing as well as could be expected; indeed, much better.

Four P.M., crossed the ferry and continued on our journey about eight or ten miles, and camped for the night at Mr. Dooly's ranch. Here we found much kindness in Mr. Dooly, much fodder for our horses, a big straw-bank for our beds, and a blue, starry sky for our roof. There was no reason, therefore, why we should not be happy. We were so; indeed, we really enjoyed our supper and our beds.

The San Joaquin plains, though the most fertile part of the state, are at this time, of course, completely dry and parched; nothing green as far as the eye can reach, except along the river banks. The crops this year have to a great extent failed, on account of the insufficient rain of the last rainy season. The only animate things which enlivened the scene this afternoon were thousands of jack-rabbits and burrowing squirrels, and their friends, the burrowing owls.

JULY 24 (SUNDAY).—*The day of rest.* Rest on the San Joaquin plains! Impossible! We pushed on this morning—this delightful, cool Sunday morning—after a refreshing night's rest. Cool in the morning, but hot, oh! how hot! as the day advanced. Made fifteen miles, and nooned at a large ranch—Mr. Ashe's. Besides the invariable jack-rabbits, burrowing squirrels, and burrowing owls, I noticed thousands of horned toads (*Phrynosoma*). I observed here a peculiarity of California life. Mr. Ashe is evidently a wealthy man. His fields are immense; his stables and barns are very ample; his horses and hired laborers are numerous; great numbers of cows, hogs, turkeys, chickens—every evidence of abundance, good living, and even of wealth, except dwelling-house. This is a shanty, scarcely fit for a cow-house. He doesn't live here, however, but in San Francisco.

I saw also today a badger. One of the party tried to shoot him, but he disappeared in a burrow.

Today has been insufferably hot. We find, upon inquiry, that there is a house at which we may stop, seven miles from this. We concluded to rest until the cool of the evening. We drowse away several hours under a wagon-shed, and resume our journey, 5:30 P.M. On the way this evening we killed two rattlesnakes, one with eight and one with twelve rattles. Enjoyed greatly the evening ride and the glorious sunset. About dark reached the house where we expected to camp; but, alas, no feed for horses! Directed to another house, two or three miles farther on. They must have feed there, for it is a *stage station*. On we went in the dark, over an exceedingly rough plowed field full of great adobe clods, and reached the house, tired and hungry, about 9 P.M. Again "No feed."

We were in despair. Impossible to go farther. "Any other house?"

"None within seven or eight miles."

When we spoke of going on, however, the main in charge (agent) hinted at the existence of a barley stack.

"That's just what we want."

"But can't let you have it."

He was evidently trying to extort from us in our necessity. This made Soulé, our Captain, so angry that he plainly told him that we would have the use of the stack, and he might get redress in any way he liked. A good deal of useless cursing passed on both sides, when, by word of command, we marched off to the stack, about one quarter-mile distant, and picketed our horses, around, with their heads to the stack. It was already so late that we did not attempt to cook supper, but ate it cold. After our cold supper, we threw ourselves upon the stack, and, although late, gazed up into the clear black sky, studded with brilliant stars, and talked for more than an hour. The young men asked me many questions about stars and nebulae and spectrum analysis, and shooting-stars and meteoric stones, which led to quite a dissertation on these subjects. The time and circumstances gave a keener interest to the discussion.

On San Joaquin plains, and, I believe, everywhere in California, however hot the days may be, the nights are delightfully cool.

JULY 25.—After a really fine night's rest, we got up about 4 A.M. The day was just breaking, and the air very clear and transparent. The blue jagged outline of the Sierra is distinctly and beautifully marked, above and beyond the nearer foot-hills, against the clear sky. In fact, there seemed to be several ridges, rising one above and beyond the other; and above and beyond all, the sharp-toothed summits of the Sierra. Took again a cold breakfast, and made an early start, 5 A.M. Went up to the house and offered to pay the agent for the barley. Charged us twenty-five dollars. We had been charged for the same everywhere else three dollars. Went into the house. Spoke to the ladies (daughters of the owner) on the subject. They were very kind and pleasant, and well satisfied with three dollars. We therefore paid them and left!

At first, our ride was delightfully pleasant in the cool morning, but gradually the bare desert plains, now monotonously rolling, became insufferably hot and dusty. The beautiful view of the Sierra, the goal of our yearnings, gradually faded away, obscured by dust, and our field of vision was again limited by the desert plains.

Journal of Ramblings

Soon after leaving the plains, we stopped for water at a neat hut, where dwelt a real *"old mammy,"* surrounded by little darkies. On inquiry I found she was from Jackson County, Georgia, and formerly owned by a Mr. Strickland. She had come to California since the war. I was really glad to see the familiar old face and hear the familiar low-country negro brogue; and she equally glad to see me. She evidently did not like California, and seemed to pine after the *"auld country."* From this place to Snelling the heat and dust were absolutely fearful. We are commencing to rise; there is no strong breeze, as on the plains; the heated air and the dust rise from the earth and envelop us, man and horse, until we can scarcely see each other. After about fifteen miles travel, arrived at Snelling at 11:30 A.M. Here we washed ourselves thoroughly, and took a good meal at the hotel, the first meal we have thus taken since leaving Oakland. We heartily enjoyed both the cleansing and the meal.

Snelling is the largest and most thriving village we have yet seen. It is in the midst of a fine agricultural district. It supplies the mining district above, without itself being entirely dependent upon that interest. Pleased to notice a very nice brick public schoolhouse. The population is probably six or seven hundred. Observed many Chinese laborers, hostlers, waiters, etc.

Continued our ride, 4 P.M., expecting to go only to Merced Falls tonight. Country beginning to be quite hilly: first, only denudation hills of drift, finely and horizontally stratified; then,

round hills, with sharp toothlike jags of perpendicularly cleaved slates, standing out thickly on
their sides. Here we first saw the auriferous
slates, and here, also, the first gravel diggings.
The auriferous gravel and pebble deposit under-
lies the soil of the valleys and ravines. About five
miles from Snelling we forded the Merced River.
Here were two roads, one along the river and
the other over the hills. Two of the young men,
Pomroy and Bolton, took the road over the hills;
the rest of us thought that along the river the
right one. Called after the other two to return;
but they thought they were right, and proceeded.
Went down the river about one half-mile below
the fall and camped. About one hour after dark,
Pomroy and Bolton returned and joined us at
supper. No straw-bank for bed tonight. On the
contrary, we camped on the barest, hardest,
and bleakest of hills, the wind sweeping up the
river over us in a perfect gale. Nevertheless, our
sleep was sound and refreshing.

I heard tonight, for the first time, of a piece of
boyish folly—to call it nothing worse—on the
part of some of the young men at Ashe's yesterday noon. While I was dozing under the shed,
some of the young men, thinking it, no doubt,
fine fun, managed to secure and appropriate
some of the poultry running about in such super-
fluous abundance in the yard. While sitting and
jotting down notes under the wagon-shed there,
I *had* observed Cobb throwing a line to some
chickens. When I looked up from my notebook,
I did observe, I now recollect, a mischievous

twinkle in his coal-black eye, and a slight quiver of his scarcely perceptible downy mustache, but I thought nothing of it. Soon after I shut up my notebook and went under a more retired shed to doze. It now appears that a turkey and several chickens had been bagged. The young rascals felicitated themselves hugely upon their good fortune; but, unfortunately, last night and this morning we made no camp-fire, and today at noon we ate at the hotel table; so that they have had no opportunity of enjoying their ill-gotten plunder until now.

Captain Soulé and myself have already expressed ourselves briefly, but very plainly, in condemnation of such conduct. Tonight the chickens were served. I said nothing, but simply, with Soulé and Hawkins, refused the delicious morsel and confined myself to bacon.

Merced Falls is a small village, deriving its importance only from a large mill situated on a rapid of the same name.

JULY 26.—Really feel quite vigorous and refreshed this morning. Got up at 4:30 A.M. Again refused fat chicken and turkey, though sorely tempted by the delicious fragrance, and ate bacon and dried beef instead. The young men have keenly felt this quiet rebuke. I feel sure this thing will not occur again. Rode, without any remarkable incident, fifteen miles this morning, to the toll-house, on the top of a high ridge. Here we nooned, fed our horses, and rested until 4 P.M. The country is becoming mountainous; we are rising the foot-hills. The soil begins to be well wooded. The air, though still hot, is more bracing. Small game is more abundant. I have become inured to the exercise of riding, and begin really to enjoy the trip. We are now on the famous Mariposa Estate. We have, all along the road today, seen abundant evidence of mining, prospecting, etc., but all abandoned. While at the toll-house, the young men amused and refreshed themselves by bathing in the horse-trough. It was really a fine bathing-tub, being about thirty feet long, two feet wide, and two feet deep, and a fine stream of water running through it. We really had a pleasant time here. Nevertheless, every joy has its corresponding sorrow. We here lost the bag containing our *cheese* and *bacon*. How it disappeared is, and probably always will be, a mystery. There are many hounds about the premises; this may furnish a key to the investigator.* The keeper of the toll-house is a rich character, a regular *Paddy*, full of fun and humor.

About 4:30 P.M. started for Mariposa, twelve miles distant. Enjoyed greatly the evening ride. Passed through the decayed, almost deserted, village of Princeton. Witnessed a magnificent sunset; brilliant golden above among the distant clouds; nearer clouds purple, shading insensibly

* Just two years after this event I again with a party passed over this road and camped overnight at this place. The hounds were still there, and we again lost our bacon. This is an additional fact in favor of the *hound theory*.

through crimson and gold into the insufferable blaze of the sun itself. Camped near an inn, where we could buy feed for our horses, one and one-half miles from Mariposa. Unfortunately, no straw-bank here, but we must lie on the hard, very hard, ground. Our bacon and cheese being lost, it is fortunate that we killed today several rabbits, quails, doves, etc., which we enjoyed at supper.

JULY 27.—After a refreshing night's rest and a hearty breakfast, we started at 6:30 A.M., and created some excitement in the town of Mariposa, by riding through the streets in double file, military fashion, and under word of command. The Captain was in his glory, and his horse seemed to sniff the battle. Dismounted at grocery-store and bought supplies. Mariposa is now greatly reduced in population and importance. It contains from five to six hundred inhabitants, but at one time two or three times that number. The same decrease is observable in all the mining towns of California. Noticed many pleasant evidences of civilization: church-spires, water-carts, fireproof stores, etc.

After about an hour's detention in Mariposa, we rode on. A little way out of town, we stopped to examine a quartz-mill. It is about forty horse-power. In the narrow, confined valleys of the foot-hills, the air is comparatively still, and the heat and dust are very great. Both horses and men very much worried by a march, this morning, of only fourteen miles. I have felt the ride much more today than yesterday. Stopped for noon meal at De Long's (near White & Hatch) half-way house from Mariposa to Clark's.

In order to avoid the heavy toll on the finely graded road to Clark's, we determined to take the very rough and steep trail over the Chowchilla Mountain, which now rose before us. My advice was to start at 3 P.M., for I still remembered Laddsville and the stage station; but the rest of the party thought the heat too great. The event proved I was right. Started 4:30 P.M. We found the trail much more difficult than we expected (we had not yet much experience in mountain trails). It seemed to pass directly up the mountain, without much regard to angle of declivity. In order to relieve our horses, we walked much of the way. Two of the party, Linderman and Cobb, stopped to refresh themselves at a deliciously cool spring. We gave them minute directions concerning the trail, and proceeded. We saw no more of them. The trail passes directly over the crest of the mountains, and down on the other side. Night overtook us when about half down. No moon; only starlight. The magnificent forests of this region, consisting of sugar-pines, yellow pines, and Douglas firs (some of the first eight to ten feet in diameter, and two hundred and fifty feet high)— grand, glorious by daylight; still grander and more glorious in the deepening shades of twilight; grandest of all by night—increased the darkness so greatly that it was impossible to see the trail.

Although in serious danger of missing footing, I could not but enjoy the night ride through those magnificent forests. These grand old trunks stand like giant sentinels about us. Were it not for our horses, I would gladly camp here in the glorious forest. But our tired horses must be fed. Down, down, winding back and forth; still down, down, down, until my back ached and my feet burned with the constant pressure on the stirrups. Still down, down, down! Is there no end? Have we not missed the trail? No Clark's yet. Down, down, down! Thus minute after minute, and, it seemed to us, hour after hour, passed away. At last the advanced guard, Hawkins, gave the Indian yell: See lights! lights! The whole company united in one shout of joy. When we arrived it was near 10 P.M. It being so late, we did not cook supper, but took supper at Clark's. Supper over, we turned our horses into Clark's meadow; selected our camp-ground, in a magnificent grove of pines one hundred and fifty to two hundred feet high; rolled ourselves in our blankets, and slept, with the mournful sighing of the pines as our lullaby.

We have felt some anxiety on account of the young men we left on the trail. After arriving at Clark's we shot off our guns and pistols, to attract their attention, thinking they might be lost on the mountains. We hope they will come in tomorrow. We killed another large rattlesnake today on the Chowchilla trail.

JULY 28.—The missing men, Linderman and Cobb, came in this morning about 10 o'clock. They had missed the trail, wandered over the mountains, reached a mountaineer's hut, been cordially received, slept overnight, and been directed on their road to Clark's this morning. Our party is complete again. Our trip thus far has been one of hardship without reward. It has been mere endurance, in the hope of enjoyment. Some enjoyment, it is true,—our camps, our morning and evening rides, our jokes, etc.,—but nothing in comparison with the dust and heat and fatigue. From this time we expect to commence the real enjoyment. We are delightfully situated here at Clark's; fine pasture for horses; magnificient grove of tall pines for camp; fine river—South Fork of Merced—to swim in; delightful air. We determined to stop here two days; one for rest and clothes-washing, and one for visiting the Big Trees. I have been sufficiently long with the party to become well acquainted with all. I have nothing to do today, except to wash my clothes. I cannot have a better opportunity to describe our party. I do it very briefly.

We are ten in number. Each man is dressed in strong trousers, heavy boots or shoes, and loose flannel shirt; a belt, with pistol and butcher-knife, about the waist; and a broad-brimmed hat. All other personal effects (and these are made as few as possible) are rolled up in a pair of blankets and securely strapped behind his saddle. Thus accoutered, we make a formidable appearance, and are taken sometimes for a troop of soldiers, but more often for a band of cattle or horse drovers. Our camp utensils consist of two large pans, to mix bread; a camp-kettle, a tea-pot, a dozen tin plates, and ten tin cups; and, most important of all, two or three frying-pans. The necessary provisions are bacon, flour, sugar, tea, and coffee. Whenever we could, we bought small quantities of butter, cheese, fresh meat, potatoes, etc. Before leaving Oakland we organized thoroughly, by electing Soulé as our Captain, and Hawkins his Lieutenant, and promised implicit obedience. This promise was strictly carried out. All important matters, however, such as our route, how long we should stay at any place, etc., was decided by vote, the Captain preferring to forgo the exercise of authority in such matters.

The names and descriptions of the members of the party are as follows:

1. *Capt. Frank Soulé.*—Strong, well-formed and straight, with clear-cut features and handsome face. Mounted on a tall, raw-boned, high-stepping dapple-gray, with a high head, a high spirit and fine action, he presents a striking appearance. He evidently feels his rank, and so does his horse. As to the latter:

> *"We shall not need to say what lack*
> *Of leather was on his back,*
> *For that was hidden under pad,*
> *And breech of Knight, galled full as bad."*

2. *Lieut. Leander Hawkins.*—Strong, thick-set, almost herculean in build. Mounted on a fierce, vicious Indian pony, as wild as a deer, which he rides with a rope around his nose, instead of a bridle, and a blind across the forehead, which may be slipped over the eyes at a moment's notice; he is evidently a most fearless rider and horse-breaker. He is, besides, thoroughly acquainted with camp life and mountain life. He is therefore the most indispensable man in the party. At first he did everything; but he has gradually taught us the mysteries of cooking, dish-washing, and, above all, packing a horse. He is also treasurer and commissary, and always rides ahead, toward evening, and selects camp-ground. Generous almost to a fault, he is ever ready to help everyone, and really does more work than any three in the party.

3. *Myself.*—Long and lean and lantern-jawed, and in search of romantic adventure, I was sometimes called by Linderman, but very secretly, "Don Quixote." I accept the nickname with pleasure, perhaps with pride. I have a great respect for the old Don. There was nothing remarkable about my horse. A strong, tough, well-made gray, both gentle and careful, he was admirably suited for my purposes. My function in the party was that of surgeon and scientific lecturer.

4. *Everett B. Pomroy.*—Short, strong, compact, muscular, with high roman nose, close-cropped hair, and coarse top-boots; very erect,

somewhat grandiose in appearance and stilted in language. He is called "Our Poet." He is

> *"A chiel amang us, takin' notes,*
> *And, faith, he'll prent it."*

He is mounted on a large, mud-colored mustang, with a broad, flat head, deep-sunk, vicious eyes, and a sprung knee. He stumbles fearfully, and bucks whenever he can, but is a tough, serviceable beast, nevertheless. We call him "Old 67," from a brand on his thigh. Pomroy sits astride of this ill-favored, hobbling beast, majestic and solemn, like Jupiter Tonans shorn of his ambrosial locks.

5. *Dell Linderman.*—Full of wit and infinite humor, quick and unfailing at repartee, with a merry twinkle in his eye, and a humorous reddish knob on the end of his nose. We call him "Our Jester." He keeps our table in a roar. All the nicknames of men and horses are of his invention. His own horse is a very stout, logy mare, with a very rough gait. He calls her "Dolly Ann, the Scabgrinder." A gun, slung over his shoulder, completes his equipment.

6. *George Cobb.*—Full of life and spirit, mercurial in temperament, with small, merry coalblack eyes, and mouth always laughing and always chattering. He rides a neat, trim, round, frisky little mare, which seems well suited to him. He carries a splendid repeating rifle, with which he oftens shoots at *marks*. He is not known to have hit any living thing. He wears,

also, neat strapped leggings. He is the fancy man and amateur sportsman of the party.

7. *Jack Bolton.*—Dark, grave, quiet; he rides a strong-boned, steady-going, grave-looking horse, of excellent gait and qualities.

8. *Charles Phelps.*—Slender, long-limbed, loose-jointed, gothic in structure of body and features, Linderman calls him "Kangaroo." His horse is a thin, slender-limbed, weak-looking mare, which in walking wobbles its hinder parts in a serpentine manner. On each side of his unsteady beast Phelp's long legs dangle in a hopeless manner.

9. *Charles Stone.*—Tall, erect; very long, curved nose; very long, straight legs, and very high hips. Linderman calls him sometimes "Crow," from his nose, and sometimes "Tongs," from his legs. His horse is a pinto iron-gray; with whitish, imbecile-looking eyes, head down, nose stuck forward, and a straddling, cowlike action of his hind legs in trotting. A tough, serviceable beast withal, except that it is impossible to cinch a saddle on his cowlike form so tightly that it will not slip on his neck in going down-hill. Linderman calls him "Samson Nipper"; why, I cannot tell; but the name seems to us all very expressive.

10. *Jim Perkins.*—A neat, trim figure, both active and strong; a fine face, with well-chiseled features; quiet, unobtrusive, gentlemanly. He was mounted on a compact, well-built horse, of excellent gait and qualities.

11. Last, but not least, is *"Old Pack,"* as we

call our pack-horse. A mild-eyed, patient, much-enduring beast, steady and careful, with every quality befitting a pack-horse. We all conceived a great affection for him.

Our party was divided into three squads of three each, leaving out Hawkins, as he helped everybody, and had more duties of his own than any of the rest. Each squad of three was on duty three days, and divided the duties of *cook*, *dishwasher*, and *pack* among themselves. On arriving at our camp-ground, each man unsaddled and picketed his horse with a long lariat rope carried on the horn of his saddle for this purpose. In addition to this, whoever attended to the pack-horse that day, unpacked him, laid the bags ready for the cook, and picketed the pack-horse. The cook then built a fire (frequently several helping, for more expedition), brought water and commenced mixing dough and baking bread. This was a serious operation, to make bread for ten, and bake in two frying-pans. First, the flour in a big pan; then yeast-powder; then salt; then mix dry; then mix with water to dough; then bake quickly; then set up before the fire to keep hot. Then use frying-pans for meat, etc. In the meantime, the *dishwash* must assist the cook by drawing tea or coffee. Our first attempts at making bread were lamentable failures. We soon found that the way to make bread was to bake from the top as well as the bottom; in fact, we often baked entirely from the top, turning it over by flipping it up in the frying-pan, and catching it on the other side. Bake, then, as follows:

Spread out the dough to fill the frying-pan, one-half inch thick, using a round stick for rolling-pin and the bottom of bread-pan for biscuit-board; set up the pan at a steep incline before the fire, by means of a stick. It is better, also, to put a few coals beneath; but this is not absolutely necessary.* It is the duty, now of the *dishwash* to set the table. For this purpose a piece of Brussels carpet (used during the day to put under the pack-saddle, but not next to the horse) is spread on the ground, and the plates and cups are arranged around. The meal is then served, and each man sits on the ground and uses his own belt-knife, and fork, if he has any. After supper we smoke, while Dishwash washes up the dishes; then we converse or sing as the spirit moves us, and then roll ourselves in our blankets, only taking off our shoes, and sleep. Sometimes we gather pine straw, leaves, or boughs, to make the ground a little less hard. In the morning, Cook and Dishwash get up early, make the fire, and commence the cooking. The rest get up a little later, in time to wash, brush hair, teeth, etc., before breakfast. We usually finish breakfast by 6 A.M. After breakfast, again wash up dishes and put away things, and deliver them to Pack, whose duty it is then to pack the pack-horse, and lead it during the day. We could travel much faster but for the pack. The pack-horse must go almost entirely in a walk; other-

* This account of bread-making anticipates a little. At this we had not yet learned to make it palatable.

wise, his pack is shaken to pieces, and his back is chafed, and we only lose time in stopping and repacking. By organizing thoroughly, dividing the duties and alternating, our party gets along in the pleasantest and most harmonious manner. After this description, I think what follows will be understood without difficulty.

Soon after breakfast this morning, Professors Church and Kendrick, of West Point, called at our camp to see Soulé and myself. Soulé had been under their tuition, and afterwards an assistant teacher at West Point. I found them very hearty and cordial in manner, very gentlemanly in spirit, polished and urbane, and, of course, very intelligent. I was really much delighted with them. They had just returned from Yosemite, and are enthusiastic in their admiration of its wonders. They are going to the Big Trees today, and return to San Francisco tomorrow. These gentlemen, of course, are not taking it in the rough way as we are. They are dressed *cap-à-pie*, and look like civilized gentlemen. They seem to admire our rough garb, and we are not at all ashamed of it.

About ten o'clock we all went down to the river, provided with soap, and washed underflannels, stockings, handkerchiefs, towels, etc. It was really a comical scene. I wish our friends in Oakland could have taken a peep—the whole party squatting on the rocks on the margin of the river, soaping and scrubbing and wringing and hanging out. After clotheswashing we took a swim in the river; then returned to camp, wrote letters home, and ate dinner.

In the afternoon, Professors Church and Kendrick again called at our camp and bade us good-by. While preparing and eating our supper, two ladies from Oakland, now staying at Clark's, friends of Phelps and Hawkins, called at our camp-fire and were introduced. They seemed much amused at our rough appearance, our crude mode of eating, and the somewhat rude manners of the young men towards one another. Their little petticoated forms, so clean and white; their gentle manners; and, above all, their sweet, smooth womanly faces, contrasted, oh! how pleasantly, with our own rough, bearded, forked appearance. They tasted some of our bread, and pronounced it excellent. Ah, the sweet, flattering, deceitful sex! It was really execrable stuff; we had not yet learned to make it palatable.

JULY 29.—Started for the Big Trees at 7 A.M. Five of the party walked, and five rode. I preferred riding, and I had no cause to regret it. The trail was very rough, and almost the whole way up-mountain; the distance about six miles, and around the grove two miles, making fourteen miles in all. The walkers were very much heated and fatigued, and drank too freely of the ice-cold water of the springs. The abundance and excessive coldness of the water seem closely connected with the occurrence of these trees.

My first impressions of the Big Trees were

somewhat disappointing; but, as I passed from one to another; as, with upturned face, I looked along their straight, polished shafts, towering to the height of three hundred feet; as I climbed up the sides of their prostrate trunks, and stepped from end to end; as I rode around the standing trees and into their enormous hollows; as we rode through the hollows of some of these prostrate trunks, and even chased one another on horseback through these enormous hollow cylinders, a sense of their immensity grew upon me. If they stood by themselves on a plain, they would be more immediately striking. But they are giants among giants. The whole forest is filled with magnificient trees, sugar-pines, yellow pines, and spruce, eight to ten feet in diameter, and two hundred to two hundred and fifty feet high. The sugar-pine, especially, is a magnificent tree in size, height, and symmetry of form.

Of all the big trees of this grove, and therefore of all the trees I have ever seen, the Grizzly Giant impressed me most profoundly; not, indeed, by its tallness or its symmetry, but by the hugeness of its cylinderical trunk, and by a certain gnarled grandeur, a fibrous, sinewy strength, which seems to defy time itself. The others, with their smooth, straight, tapering shafts, towering to the height of three hundred feet, seemed to me the type of youthful vigor and beauty in the plenitude of power and success. But *this*, with its large, rough, knobbed, battered trunk, more than thirty feet in diameter—with top broken off and decayed at the height of one hundred and fifty feet—with its great limbs, six to eight feet in diameter, twisted and broken—seemed to me the type of a great life, decaying, but still strong and self-reliant. Perhaps my own bald head and grizzled locks—my own top, with its decaying foliage—made me sympathize with this grizzled giant; but I found the Captain, too, standing with hat in hand, and gazing in silent, bare-headed reverence upon the grand old tree.

We lunched at the Big Trees, rested, examined them three or four hours, and then returned to camp. Then went down to the creek, and enjoyed a delicious swimming-bath. On the way back to camp, stopped at Clark's, and became acquainted with President Mark Hopkins and his family. He goes to Yosemite tomorrow. We will see him again. After supper, the young men, sitting under the tall pines, sang in chorus. The two ladies already spoken of, hearing the music, came down to our camp, sat on the ground, and joined in the song. Cobb's noisy tenor, fuller of spirit than music, Pomroy's bellowing baritone, and, especially, Stone's deep, rich, really fine bass, harmonized very pleasantly with the thin clearness of the feminine voices. I really enjoyed the song and the scene very greatly. Women's faces and women's voices, after our rough life, and contrasted with our rough forms—ah! how delightful! About 9:30 P.M. they left, and we all turned in for the night. For an hour I lay upon my back, gazing upwards through the tall pines into the dark starry sky, which seemed almost to rest on their tops, and listening to the solemn murmurings of their leaves, which, in the silent night, seemed like the whisperings of spirits of the air above me.

JULY 30.—Got up at 4 A.M. My turn to play cook. But cooking for ten hungry men, in two frying-pans, is no play. It requires both time and patience. We did not get off until 7 A.M. Captain not very well today—too much violent exercise and ice-cold water yesterday. Another bucking farce this morning. Captain's horse, it seems, has more style and spirit than bottom. He has become badly galled, and has been a constant source of annoyance to the Captain since we left. He therefore concluded to leave his horse here at Clark's, to "heal him of his grievous wounds," and hire a mule—at least while we remain at Yosemite. He no sooner mounted than the mule started off in the contrary direction, kicking and plunging and jumping stiff-legged, until he threw off—not the Captain, indeed, but the pack behind the saddle.

After some delay, however, we started off fairly. No more roads hereafter; only steep, rough mountain trails. We are heartily glad, for we have no dust. President Hopkins and party started off with us. His party consisted of himself, wife, son, and several other ladies and gentlemen, and a guide, numbering in all eight. Our party numbered ten and pack. Together, we made a formidable cavalcade. The young men were in high spirits. They sang and hallooed and cracked jokes the whole way. Rode twelve miles, up-hill nearly all the way, and camped for noon at Westfall's Meadows, over seven thousand feet above sea-level. Hopkins' party went on a mile or two, to Peregoy's (the half-way house to Yosemite), to lunch. In this party is a short, stout, round-faced, laughing-eyed rather pretty young woman, in very short bloomer costume, which shows a considerable portion of two very fat legs. Her bloomer makes her look still more squat; and to make things worse, she cannot forgo the fashionable bunch of knots and bows and ribbons on or below the waist, behind. Altogether, she was an amusing figure. Our young men called her "Miss Bloomer." The Captain, I think, is struck, but he worships, as yet, only at a distance.

In the afternoon we pushed on, to get our first view of Yosemite this evening, from Sentinel Dome and Glacier Point. Passing Peregoy's, I saw a rough-looking man standing in an open place, with easel on thumb, and canvas before him, alternatively gazing on the fine mountain view and painting.

"Hello! Mr. Tracy, glad to see you."

"Why, Doctor, how do you do? Where are you going?"

"Yosemite, the High Sierra, Lake Mono, and Lake Tahoe."

"Ah! how I wish I could go with you!"

After a few such pleasant words of greeting and inquiry, I galloped on, and overtook our party on the trail to Glacier Point. About 5 P.M. we passed a high pile of rocks, called Os-

trander's Rocks. The whole trail, from Westfall's Meadows to Glacier Point, is near eight
thousand feet high. From this rocky prominence,
therefore, the view is really magnificent. It was
our first view of the peaks and domes about
Yosemite, and of the more distant High Sierra,
and we enjoyed it beyond expression. But there
are still finer views ahead, which we must see
this afternoon—yes, this very afternoon. With
increasing enthusiasm we pushed on until, about
6 P.M., we reached and climbed Sentinel Dome.
This point is 4,500 feet above Yosemite Valley,
and 8,500 feet above the sea.

The view which here burst upon us, of the
valley and the Sierra, it is simply impossible to
describe. Sentinel Dome stands on the south
margin of Yosemite, near the point where it
branches into three cañons. To the left stand El
Capitan's massive perpendicular wall; directly
in front, and distant about one mile, Yosemite
Falls, like a gauzy veil, rippling and waving with
a slow, mazy motion; to the right the mighty
granite mass of Half Dome lifts itself in solitary
grandeur, defying the efforts of the climber; to
the extreme right, and a little behind, Nevada
Fall, with the Cap of Liberty; in the distance,
innumerable peaks of the High Sierra, conspicuous among which are Clouds Rest, Mt. Starr
King, Cathedral Peak, etc. We remained on the
top of this dome more than an hour, to see the
sunset. We were well repaid—such a sunset I
never saw; such a sunset, combined with such
a view, I had never imagined. The glorious golden

and crimson in the west, and the exquisitely delicate diffused rose-bloom, tingeing the cloud caps of the Sierra in the east, and the shadows of the grand peaks and domes slowly creeping up the valley! I can never forget the impression. We remained, enjoying this scene, too long to think of going to Glacier Point this evening. We therefore put this off until morning, and returned on our trail about one and a half miles, to a beautiful green meadow (Hawkins had chosen it on his way to Sentinel Dome), and there made camp in a grove of magnificent fir trees (*Abies magnifica*).*

JULY 31 (SUNDAY).—I got up at peep of day this morning (I am dishwash today), roused the party, started a fire, and in ten minutes tea was ready. All partook heartily of this delicious beverage, and started on foot to see the sunrise from Glacier Point. This point is about one and a half miles from our camp, about 3,200 feet above the valley, and forms the salient angle on the south side, just where the valley divides into three. We had to descend about eight hundred feet to reach it. We arrived just before sunrise. Sunrise from Glacier Point! No one can appreciate it who has not seen it. It was our good fortune to have an exceedingly beautiful sunrise. Rosy-fingered Aurora revealed herself to us, her votaries, more bright and charming and rosy

* The original edition reads: "Spruce trees (*Picea Grandis*)," corrected in the edition of 1900.—EDITOR.

than ever before. But the great charm was the view of the valley and surrounding peaks, in the fresh, cool morning hour and in the rosy light of the rising sun; the bright, warm light on the mountaintops, and the cool shade in the valley. The shadow of the grand Half Dome stretches clear across the valley, while its own "bald, awful head" glitters in the early sunlight. To the right, Vernal and Nevada falls, with their magnificent overhanging peaks, in full view; while directly across, see the ever-rippling, ever-swaying gauzy veil of the Yosemite Falls, reaching from top to bottom of the opposite cliff, 2,600 feet. Below, at a depth of 3,200 feet, the bottom of the valley lies like a garden. There, right under our noses, are the hotels, the orchards, the fields, the meadows (near one of these Hawkins even now selects our future camp), the forests, and through all the Merced River winds its apparently lazy serpentine way. Yonder, up the Tenaya Cañon, nestling close under the shadow of Half Dome, lies Mirror Lake, fast asleep, her polished black surface not yet ruffled by the rising wind. I have heard and read much of this wonderful valley, but I can truly say I have never imagined the grandeur of the reality. After about one and a half hours' rapturous gaze, we returned to camp and breakfasted. I had left Glacier Point a few minutes before most of the party, as I was dishwash, and had, therefore, to help cook prepare breakfast. At breakfast I learned that two of the young men, Cobb and Perkins, had undertaken the foolish enterprise of going down into the valley by a cañon just below Glacier Point, and returning by 4 P.M. Think of it! 3,300 feet perpendicular, and the declivity, it seemed to me, about forty-five degrees in the cañon!

After breakfast we returned to Glacier Point and spent the whole of the beautiful Sunday morning in the presence of grand mountains, yawning chasms, and magnificent falls. What could we do better than allow these to preach to us? Was there ever so venerable, majestic, and eloquent a minister of natural religion as the grand old Half Dome? I withdrew myself from the rest of the party and drank in his silent teachings for several hours. About 1 P.M. climbed Sentinel Dome and enjoyed again the matchless panoramic view from this point, and about 2 P.M. returned to camp.

Our camp is itself about four thousand feet above the valley, and eight thousand above sea-level. By walking about one hundred yards from our camp-fire, we get a most admirable view of the Sierra, and particularly a most wonderfully striking view of the unique form of Half Dome when seen in profile. I enjoyed this view until nearly time to saddle up.

Our plan is to return to Peregoy's, only seven miles, this afternoon, and go to Yosemite to-morrow morning. It is 3:30 P.M., and the young men who went down into the valley have not yet returned. We feel anxious. Will they return, or remain in the valley? Shall we remain tonight and wait for them, or go on, leading their horses, with the expectation of meeting them in the valley? We are to leave at four; we must decide soon. These discussions were cut short by the appearance of the delinquents themselves, faint with fatigue. They had been down, taken dinner, and returned. We started immediately for Peregoy's, where we arrived, 6 P.M., and camped in a grove on the margin of a fine meadow. At Peregoy's we bought a quarter of mountain mutton. We have been living on bacon and bread for some time. The voracity with which we devoured that mutton may be more easily imagined than described.

Ever since we have approached the region of the High Sierra, I have observed the great massiveness and grandeur of the clouds and the extreme blueness of the sky. In the direction of the Sierra hang always magnificent piles of snow-white cumulus, sharply defined against the deep-blue sky. These cloud-masses have ever been my delight. I have missed them sadly since coming to California, until this trip. I now welcome them with joy. Yesterday and today I have seen, in many places, snow lying on the northern slopes of the high peaks of the Sierra.

AUGUST 1.—*Yosemite today!* Started as usual, 7 A.M. President Hopkins and family go with us. They had stayed at Peregoy's over Sunday. I think we kept Sunday better. Glorious ride this morning through the grand fir forests. This is enjoyment, indeed. The trail is tolerably good until it reaches the edge of the Yosemite chasm. On the trail a little way below this edge there is a jutting point, called "Inspiration Point," which gives a good general view of the lower end of the valley, including El Capitan, Cathedral Rock, and a glimpse of Bridalveil Fall. After taking this view we began the descent into the valley. The trail winds backward and forward on the almost perpendicular sides of the cliff, making a descent of about three thousand feet in three miles. It was so steep and rough that we preferred walking most of the way and leading the horses. Poor old Mrs. Hopkins, though a heavy old lady, was afraid to ride, and therefore walked the whole way. At last, 10 A.M., we were down, and the gate of the valley is before us, El Capitan guarding it on the left and Cathedral Rock on the right, while over the precipice on the right the silvery gauze of Bridalveil is seen swaying to and fro.

We encamped in a fine forest on the margin of Bridalveil Meadow, under the shadow of El Capitan, and about one-quarter of a mile from Bridalveil Fall. Turned our horses loose to graze, cooked our midday meal, refreshed ourselves by swimming in the Merced, and then, 4:30 P.M., started to visit Bridalveil. We had understood that this was the best time to see it. Very difficult clambering to the foot of the fall up a steep incline, formed by a pile of huge boulders fallen from the cliff. The enchanting beauty and exquisite grace of this fall well repaid us for the toil. At the base of the fall there is a beautiful pool. Standing on the rocks on the margin of this pool, right opposite the fall, a most perfect unbroken circular rainbow is visible. Sometimes it is a double circular rainbow. The cliff more than six hundred feet high; the wavy, billowy, gauzy veil reaching from top to bottom; the glorious crown, woven by the sun for this beautiful veiled bride—those who read must put these together and form a picture for themselves by the plastic power of the imagination.

Some of the young men took a swim in the pool and a shower-bath under the fall. I would have joined them, but I had just come out of the Merced River. After enjoying this exquisite fall until after sunset, we returned to camp. On our way back, amongst the loose rocks on the stream margin, we found and killed another rattlesnake. This is the fourth we have killed.

Hawkins, the enterprising and indefatigable, has been today up to the hotel for supplies. He has returned, bringing among other things a quarter of mutton and two pounds of butter. These, with a due amount of bread, etc., scarcely stayed our fierce appetites. After supper we lit cigarettes, gathered around the campfire, and conversed. Some question of the relative merits of novelists was started, and my opinion asked. By repeated questions I was led into quite a disquisition on art and literature, which lasted until bedtime. Before retiring, as usual, we piled huge logs on the camp-fire; then rolled ourseves in our blankets within reach of its warmth.

Forming part of the cliff, at the base of Bridalveil Fall, I observed a remarkable mass of dark rock, like diorite, veined in the most complicated manner with whitish granite. In some places the granite predominates, and incloses isolated masses of diorite.

August 2.—Started this morning up the valley. As we go, the striking features of Yosemite pass in procession before us. On the left, El Capitan, Three Brothers, Yosemite Falls; on the right, Cathedral Rock, Cathedral Spires, Sentinel Rock. Cathedral Spires really strongly remind one of a huge cathedral, with two tall equal spires five hundred feet high, and several smaller ones. I was reminded of old Trinity, in Columbia. But *this* was not made with hands, and is over two thousand feet high. Stopped at Hutchings' and took lunch. Here I received letters from home. All well, thank God! Here again met President Hopkins and party; also, our friend Miss Bloomer greeted us merrily. Soulé seems deeply smitten, poor fellow! We here had our party photographed in costume. The photographer is none of the best; but we hope the picture will be a pleasure to our friends in Oakland.

We first tried it on horseback, but found it impossible. We must be content to leave out these noble animals. Captain is secretly glad— he has left his high-stepping gray at Clark's, and now bestrides a sorry mule. Those ears, he thinks, don't look martial. Now then, for a striking group!

As the most venerable of the party, my position was in the middle, and my bald head, glistening in the sunshine, was supposed to give dignity to the group. I was supported on either hand by Captain and Perkins, as the handsomest. Dignity supported by beauty — fitting union! Beyond these, on one side stood grave Bolton, in stiff attitude, with his hand resting on Hawkins' gun; while on the other, Linderman, with broad-brimmed hat thrown back, and chest thrown forward, and his gun strapped across his back, tried in vain to make his humorous face look fierce. On the extreme wings, Cobb with his inevitable rifle, and Phelps with his loose-jointed legs, struck each a tragic attitude. In the foreground, at our feet, were placed the other three. Hawkins' burly bulk, in careless position, occupied the middle, while Pomroy gave solemnity to the left; and on the right, Stone, reclining on his elbow, gathered up his long legs to bring them, if possible, within the view of the great eye of the camera, and placed his broad-brim on his knee, in vain attempts to conceal "their utmost longitude." Far in the background was the granite wall of Yosemite, and the wavy white waters of the falls. The result is seen in the photograph of the University Excursion Party in Yosemite Valley (*see* photo section).

In the afternoon went on up the valley, and again the grand procession commences. On the left, Royal Arches, Washington Column, North Dome; on the right, Sentinel Dome, Glacier Point, Half Dome. We pitched our camp in a magnificent forest, near a grassy meadow (the same Hawkins had selected from Glacier Point yesterday) on the banks of Tenaya Fork, and under the shadow of our venerated preacher and friend, the Half Dome, with also North Dome, Washington Column, and Glacier Point in full view.

After unsaddling and turning loose our horses to graze, and resting a little, we went up the Tenaya Cañon about one and a half miles, to Mirror Lake, and took a swimming bath. The scenery about this lake is truly magnificent. The cliffs of Yosemite here reach the acme of imposing grandeur. On the south side the broad face of South Dome rises almost from the water, a sheer precipice near five thousand feet perpendicular; on the north side, North Dome, with its finely rounded head, to an almost equal height. Down the cañon, to the west, the view is blocked by the immense cliffs of Glacier Point and Washington Column; and up the cañon, to the east, the cliffs of the Tenaya Cañon and the Clouds Rest, and the peaks of the Sierra in the background. On returning to camp, as we expected to remain here for several days, we carried with us a number of "shakes" (split boards), and constructed a very good table, around which we placed logs for seats. We cooked our supper, sat around our rude board, and enjoyed our meal immensely.

After supper, sat around our camp-fire, smoked our cigarettes, and sang in chorus until 9:30 P.M., then rolled ourselves, chrysalis-like, in our blanket cocoons, and lay still until morning.

Already I observed two very distinct kinds of structure in the granite of this region, which, singly or combined, determine all the forms about this wonderful valley. These two kinds of structure are the concentric structure, on an almost inconceivably grand scale, and a rude columnar structure, or perpendicular cleavage, also on a grand scale. The disintegration and exfoliation of the granite masses of the concentric structures give rise to the bald rounded domes; the structure itself is well seen on Sentinel Dome, and especially in the Royal Arches. The columnar structure, by disintegration, gives rise to Washington Column and the sharp peaks, like Sentinel Rock and Cathedral Spires. Both these structures exist in the same granite, though the one or the other may predominate. In *all* the rocks about Yosemite there is a tendency to cleave perpendicularly. In addition to this, in many there is also a tendency to cleave in concentric layers, giving rise to dome-like forms. Both are well seen combined in the grand mass of Half Dome. The perpendicular face-wall of this dome is the result of the perpendicular cleavage. Whatever may be our theory of the formation of Yosemite chasm and the perpendicularity of its cliffs, we must not leave out of view this tendency to perpendicular cleavage. I observe, too, that the granite here is very coarse-grained, and disintegrates into dust with great rapidity.

I observed, today, the curious straw- and grass-covered stacks in which the Indians store and preserve their supplies of acorns.

August 3.—This has been to me a day of intense enjoyment. Started off this morning, with six others of the party, to visit Vernal and Nevada falls. There are many Indians in the valley. We do not think it safe to leave our camp.* We therefore divide our party every day, a portion keeping guard. Soulé Phelps, and and Perkins were camp-guard today.

The Vernal and Nevada falls are formed by the Merced River itself; the volume of water, therefore, is very considerable in all seasons. The surrounding scenery, too, is far finer, I think, than that of any other fall in the valley. The trail is steep and very rough, ascending nearly two thousand feet to the foot of Nevada Fall. To the foot of Vernal Fall, the trail passes through dense woods, close along the banks of the Merced, which here rushes down its steep channel, forming a series of rapids and cascades of enchanting beauty. We continued our way on horseback until it seemed almost impossible

---

* We learned afterwards that we might have left the camp unguarded with perfect safety.

for horses to go any farther; we then dismounted, unsaddled and hitched our horses, and proceeded on foot. We afterwards discovered that we had already gone over the worst part of the trail to the foot of Vernal Fall before we hitched; we should have continued on horseback to the refreshment cabin at the foot of Vernal Fall. We arrived at the refreshment cabin very much heated, and took some refreshment before proceeding.

Here we again saw the bright face, the laughing eyes, and fat legs of Miss Bloomer, which were also a very great refreshment. Alas for Captain! he is not with us today.

The Vernal Fall is an absolutely perpendicular fall of four hundred feet, surrounded by the most glorious scenery imaginable. The exquisite greenness of the trees, the grass, and the moss renders the name peculiarly appropriate. The top of the fall is reached by step-ladder, which ascends the absolutely perpendicular face of the precipice. From the top the view is far grander than from below; for we take in the fall and the surrounding scenery at one view. An immense natural parapet of rock rises, breast-high, above the general surface of the cliff, near the fall. Here one can stand securely, leaning on the parapet, and enjoy the magnificent view. The river pitches, at our very feet, over a precipice four hundred feet high, into a narrow gorge, bounded on either side by cliffs such as are seen nowhere except in Yosemite, and completely blocked in front by the massive cliffs of Glacier Point, 3,200 feet high; so that it actually seems to pitch into an amphitheater, with rocky walls higher than its diameter. Oh, the glory of the view!—the emerald green and snowy white of the falling water; the dizzying leap into the yawning chasm; the roar and foam and spray of the deadly struggle with rocks below; the deep green of the somber pines, and the exquisitely fresh and lively green of grass, ferns, and moss, wet with eternal spray; the perpendicular rocky walls, rising far above us toward the blue arching sky. As I stood there, gazing down into the dark and roaring chasm, and up into the clear sky, my heart swelled with gratitude to the Great Author of all beauty and grandeur.

After enjoying this view until we could spare no more time, we went on about one-half mile to the foot of Nevada Fall. Mr. Pomroy and myself mistook the trail and went up the left side of the river to the foot of the fall. To attain this point we had to cross two roaring cataracts under circumstances of considerable danger, at least to any but those who possess steady nerves. We finally succeeded in clambering to the top of a huge boulder twenty feet high, immediately in front of the fall, and only thirty or forty feet from it. Here, stunned by the roar and blinded by the spray, we felt the full power and grandeur of the fall. From this place we saw, and greeted with Indian yell, our companions on the other side of the river. After remaining here an hour, we went a little down

The University Excursion Party in Yosemite Valley:
Phelps, Bolton, Perkins, Prof. LeConte, Soulé,
Linderman, Cobb, Stone, Hawkins, Pomroy.

The Grizzly Giant;
110 feet in circumference, 33 feet in diameter.

The High Sierra from Glacier Point.

The Gates of the Valley from Inspiration Point.

Bridalveil Fall.

Day-dawn in Yosemite: the Merced River.

The heart of the Sierra: Lake Tenaya.

In Yosemite Valley: Linderman, Cobb, Bolton

Montgomery Street, San Francisco—where our trip ended.

the stream and crossed to the other side, and again approached the fall. The view from this, the right side, is the one usually taken. It is certainly the finest scenic view, but the power of falling water is felt more grandly from the nearer view on the other side. The lover of intense ecstatic emotion will prefer the latter; the lover of quiet scenic beauty will prefer the former. The poet will seek inspiriation in the one, and the painter in the other.

The Nevada Fall is, I think, the grandest I have ever seen. The fall is six hundred to seven hundred feet high. It is not an absolutely perpendicular leap, like Vernal, but is all the grander on that account; as, by striking several ledges in its downward course, it is beaten into a volume of snowy spray, ever changing in form, and impossible to describe. From the same cause, too, it has a slight S-like curve which is exquisitely graceful. But the magnificence of the Yosemite cascades, especially of Vernal and Nevada falls, is due principally to the accompanying scenery. See Cap of Liberty and its fellow peak, rising perpendicular, tall and sharp, until actually (I speak without exaggeration) the intense blue sky and masses of white clouds seem to rest supported on their summits. The actual height above the fall is, I believe, about two thousand feet.

About 3 P.M. started on our return. There is a beautiful pool, about three hundred feet long and one hundred and fifty to two hundred feet wide, immediately above the Vernal Fall. Into this pool the Merced River rushes as a foaming rapid, and leaves it only to precipitate itself over the precipice, as the Vernal Fall. The fury with which the river rushes down a steep incline, into the pool, creates waves like the sea. On returning, all of us who were good swimmers refreshed ourselves by swimming in this pool. I enjoyed the bath immensely; swam across, played among the waves, contended with the swift current, shouted and laughed like the veriest boy of them all. The water was of course very cold, but we have become accustomed to this. On coming out of my bath, I took one final look over the rocky parapet, over the fall, and into the yawning chasm below.

Returned to camp at 5 P.M., fresh and vigorous, and with a keen appetite for supper. After enjoying that most important meal, as usual, we gathered around our camp-fire, sat on the ground, and the young men sang in chorus.

AUGUST 4.—This has been to me an uneventful day; I stayed in camp today as one of the camp-guard, while the camp-guard of yesterday visited the Vernal and Nevada falls. I have lolled about camp, writing letters home, sewing on buttons, etc.; but most of the time in a sort of day-dream —a glorious day-dream in the presence of this grand nature. Ah! this free life in the presence of great Nature is indeed delightful! There is but one thing greater in this world—one thing after which, even under the shadow of this grand wall of rock, upon whose broad face and summit-line projected against the clear blue sky with up-turned face I now gaze; one thing after which even now I sigh with inexpressible longing—and that is Home and Love. A loving human heart is greater and nobler even than the grand scenery of Yosemite. In the midst of the grandest scenes of yesterday, while gazing alone upon the falls and the stupendous surrounding cliffs, my heart filled with gratitude to God and love to the dear ones at home; my eyes involuntarily over-flowed, and my hands clasped in silent prayer.

In the afternoon we took our usual swim in the Mirror Lake; after which, of course, supper and bed.

AUGUST 5.—Today to Yosemite Falls. This was the hardest day's experience yet. We thought we had plenty of time, and therefore started late. Stopped a moment at the foot of the falls, at a saw-mill, to make inquiries. Here found a man in rough miller's garb, whose intelligent face and earnest, clear blue eye excited my interest. After some conversation, discovered that it was Mr. Muir, a gentleman of whom I had heard much from Mrs. Professor Carr and others. He had also received a letter from Mrs. Carr concerning our party, and was looking for us. We were glad to meet each other. I urged him to go with us to Mono, and he seemed disposed to do so.

We first visited the foot of the lower fall, which is about four hundred feet perpendicular, and after enjoying it for a half-hour or more, returned to the mill. It was now nearly noon.

Impossible to undertake the difficult ascent to the upper fall without lunch; I therefore jumped on the first horse I could find (mine was unsaddled) and rode to Mr. Hutchings' and took a hearty lunch, to which Mr. Hutchings insisted upon adding a glass of generous California wine. On returning, found the rest of the party at the mill. On learning my good fortune, they also went and took lunch.

We now commenced the ascent. We first clambered up a mere pile of loose débris (talus), four hundred feet high, and inclined at least forty-five to fifty degrees. We had to keep near to one another, for the boulders were constantly loosened by the foot and went bounding down the incline until they reached the bottom. Heated and panting, we reach the top of the lower fall, drank, and plunged our heads in the foaming water until thoroughly refreshed. After remaining here nearly an hour, we commenced the ascent to the foot of the upper fall. Here the clambering was the most difficult and precarious I have ever tried; sometimes climbing up perpendicular rock faces, taking advantage of cracks and clinging bushes; sometimes along joint-cracks, on the dizzy edge of fearful precipices; sometimes over rock faces so smooth and highly inclined that we were obliged to go on hands and knees. In many places a false step would be fatal. There was no trail at all; only piles of stones here and there to mark the best route. But when at last we arrived we were amply repaid for our labor. Imagine a sheer cliff, sixteen hundred feet high, and a stream pouring over it. Actually, the water

seems to fall out of the very sky itself. As I gaze
upward now, there are wisps of snowy cloud
just on the verge of the precipice above; the white
spray of the washing cataract hangs, also, apparently almost motionless on the same verge. It is
difficult to distinguish wisps of spray from wisps
of cloud, so long a column of water and spray
is swayed from side to side by the wind; and,
also, as in all falls, the resistance of the rocks
at the top, and of the air, in the whole descent,
produces a billowy motion. The combination of
these two motions, both so conspicuous in this
fall, is inexpressibly graceful. When the column
swayed far to the left, we ran by on the right,
and got behind the fall, and stood gazing through
the gauzy veil upon the cliffs on the opposite
side of the valley. At this season of the year the
Yosemite Creek is much diminished in volume.
It strikes slightly upon the face of the cliff, about
midway up. In the spring and autumn, when the
river is full, the fall must be grand indeed. It
is then a clear leap of sixteenth hundred feet,
and the pool which it has hollowed out for itself
in the solid granite is plainly visible twenty to
thirty feet in advance of the place on which it
now falls.

We met here, at the foot of the fall, a real
typical specimen of a live Yankee. He has, he
says, a panorama of Yosemite, which he expects
to exhibit in the Eastern cities. It is evident that
he is "doing" Yosemite only for the purpose of
getting materials of lectures to accompany his
exhibitions.

Coming down in the afternoon the fatigue was

less, but the danger much greater. We were often compelled to slide down the face of rocks in a sitting posture, to the great detriment of the posterior portion of our trousers. Reached bottom at half-past five P.M. Here learned from Mr. Muir that he would certainly go to Mono with us. We were much delighted to hear this. Mr. Muir is a gentleman of rare intelligence, of much knowledge of science, particularly of botany, which he has made a specialty. He has lived several years in the valley, and is thoroughly acquainted with the mountains in the vicinity. A man of so much intelligence tending a sawmill!— not for himself, but for Mr. Hutchings. This is California!

After arranging our time of departure from Yosemite with Mr. Muir, we rode back to camp. I enjoyed greatly the ride to camp, in the cool of the evening. The evening view of the valley was very fine, and changing at every step. Just before reaching our camp, there is a partial distant view of the Illilouette Fall—the only one I know of in the valley. Many of the party seem wearied this evening. For myself, I feel fresh and bright. We were all, however, sound asleep by 8 P.M.*

---

* Our party did not visit the Illilouette Fall, but on a subsequent trip to Yosemite I did so. The following is a brief description, taken from my journal, which I introduce here in order to complete my account of the falls of this wondrous valley:

AUGUST 15, 1872.—Started with Mr. Muir and my nephew Julian to visit Illilouette Fall. Hearing that there was no trail, and that the climb is more difficult even than that to the Upper Yosemite, the rest of the party *backed out*. We rode up the Merced, on the Vernal Fall trail, to the junction of the Illilouette Fork. Here we secured our horses and proceeded on foot up the cañon. The rise, from this to the foot of the fall, is twelve hundred to fifteen hundred feet. The whole cañon is literally filled with huge rock fragments—often hundreds of tons in weight—brought down from the cliffs at the fall. The scramble up the steep ascent over these boulders was extremely difficult and fatiguing. Oftentimes the creek-bed was utterly impracticable, and we had to climb high up the sides of the gorge and down again. But we were gloriously repaid for our labor. There are beauties about this fall which are peculiar and simply incomparable. It was to me a new experience and a peculiar joy. The volume of water, when I saw it, was several times greater than either Yosemite or Bridalveil. The stream plunges into a narrow chasm, bounded on three sides by perpendicular walls nearly one thousand feet high. The height of the fall is six hundred feet. Like Nevada, the fall is not absolutely perpendicular, but strikes about half-way down on the face of the cliff. But instead of striking on projecting ledges and being thus *beaten* into a great volume of foam, as in the latter, it *glides* over the somewhat even surface of the rock, and is *woven* into the most exquisite lacework, with edging fringe and pendent tassels, ever-changing and ever-delighting. It is simply impossible even to conceive, much less to describe, the exquisite delicacy and tantalizing beauty of the ever-changing forms. The effect produced is not tumultuous excitement, or ecstacy, like Nevada, but simple, pure, almost childish delight. Now as I sit on a great boulder twenty feet high, right in front of the fall, see! the midday sun shoots its beams through the myriad water-draps which leap from the top of the cascade as it strikes the edge of the cliff. As I gaze upwards, the glittering drops seem to pause a moment high in the air and then descend like a glorious star-shower.

AUGUST 6.—Slept late this morning. Some of the party stiff and sore; I am all right. The camp-guard of yesterday visited Yosemite Falls today, and we stayed in camp. Visited Mirror Lake this morning to see the fine reflection of the surrounding cliffs in its unruffled waters in the early morning. Took a swim in the lake; spent the rest of the morning washing clothes, writing letters, and picking and eating raspberries in Lamon's garden.

To a spectator the clothes-washing forms a very interesting scene. To see us all sitting down on the rocks, on the banks of the beautiful Tenaya River, scrubbing and wringing and hanging out! It reminds one of the exquisite washing scene of Princess Nausicaa and her damsels, or of Pharaoh's daughter and her maids. Change the sex, and where is the inferiority in romantic interest in our case? Ah! *the sex!* yes, this makes all the difference between the ideal and common —between poetry and prose. If it were only seven beautiful women, in simple attire, and I, like Ulysses, a spectator just waked from sleep by their merry peals of laughter! But seven rough, bearded fellows!—think of it! We looked about us, but found no little Moses in the bulrushes. So we must e'en take Mr. Muir and Hawkins to lead us through the wilderness of the High Sierra!

In the afternoon we moved camp to our previous camping-ground at Bridalveil Meadow. We were really sorry to break up our camp on Tenaya Creek. We have had delightful times here.

We called it *University Camp*. Soon after leaving camp, Soulé and myself, riding together, heard a hollow rumbling, then a crashing sound. "Is it thunder or earthquake?" Looking up quickly, the white streak down the cliff of Glacier Point, and the dust there rising from the valley, revealed the fact that it was the falling of a huge rock mass from Glacier Point.

We rode down in the cool of the evening, and by moonlight. Took leave of our friends *in* the valley—McKee and his party, Mr. and Mrs. Hutchings, Mrs. Yelverton, Miss Bloomer (whom we again met, and with whom Captain exchanged photographs); sad leave of our friends, now dear friends, *of* the valley: the venerable and grand old South Dome, under whose shadow we had camped so long; North Dome, Washington Column, Royal Arches, Glacier Point; then Yosemite Falls, Sentinel Rock, Three Brothers.

By this time night had closed in; but the moon was near full, and the shadows of Cathedral Spires and Cathedral Rock lay across our path, while the grand rock mass of El Capitan shone gloriously white in the moonlight. The ride was really enchanting to all, but affected us differently. The young men rode ahead, singing in chorus. I lagged behind, and enjoyed it in silence. The choral music, mellowed by distance, seemed to harmonize with the scene and to enhance its holy stillness.

About half-past 8 P.M. we encamped on the western side of Bridalveil Meadow. After supper we were in fine spirits, contended in gymnastic exercises, etc. Then gathered hay, made a delightful fragrant bed, and slept dreamlessly.

At Mr. Hutchings' I again received letters from home—very happy to know that they are well.

AUGUST 7 (SUNDAY).—Got up late—6 A.M.—as is common everywhere on this day of rest. Now, about to leave for Mono, Captain must have his horse or he cannot accompany us. He only hired the mule while in Yosemite. Mr. Perkins volunteered to ride the mule back to Clark's and bring Captain's horse. He started very early this morning, and hopes to be back by bedtime.

About 11 A.M. took a quiet swim in the river; for we think a *clean skin* is next in importance to a *pure heart*. During the rest of the morning I sat and enjoyed the fine view of the opening, or gate, of the valley, from the lower side of the meadow. There stands the grand old El Capitan in massive majesty on the left, and Cathedral Rock and the Veiled Bride on the right. I spent the morning with this scene before me. While sitting here I again took out my little sewing-case and darned my trousers, a little broken by my experiments in sliding day before yesterday. God bless the dear thoughtful one who provided me with this necessary article! God bless the little fingers which arranged these needles and wound so neatly the thread; May God's choicest blessings rest on the dear ones at home! May He, the Infinite Love, keep them in health and happiness until I return! Surely, absence from home is sometimes necessary to make us feel the priceless value of loving hearts.

There is considerable breeze to-day; and now, while I write, the Bride's veil is wafted from side to side, and sometimes lifted until I can almost see the blushing face of the Bride herself—the beautiful spirit of the fall. But whose bride? Is it old El Capitan? Strength and grandeur united with grace and beauty! Fitting union!

At 3 P.M. went again alone to the lower side of the meadow and sat down before the gate of the valley. From this point I look directly through the gate and up the valley. There again, rising to the very skies, stands the huge mass of El Capitan on one side, and on the other the towering peak of the Cathedral, with the Veiled Bride retiring a little back from the too ardent gaze of admiration; then the cliffs of Yosemite, growing narrower and lower on each side, beyond. Conspicuous, far in the distance, see! old South Dome and Clouds Rest. The sky is perfectly serene, except heavy masses of snow-white cumulus, sharply defined against the deep blue of the sky, filling the space beyond the gate. The wavy motion of the Bride's veil, as I gaze steadfastly upon it, drowses my sense; I sit in a kind of delicious dream, the scenery unconsciously mingling with my dream.

Five P.M. Went, all of us, this afternoon to visit the Bride. Saw again the glorious crown set by the sun upon her beautiful head. Swam in the pool at her feet. Tried to get a peep beneath the veil, but got pelted beyond endurance with water-drops, by the little fairies which guard her beauty, for my sacrilegious rudeness. Nevertheless, came back much exhilarated, and feeling more like a boy than I had felt for many, many years.

Perkins returned with Captain's horse, to supper.

Eight P.M. After supper, went again alone into the meadow to enjoy the moonlight view. The moon is long risen, and "near her highest noon," but not yet visible in this deep valley, although I am sitting on the extreme northern side, Cathedral Rock and the snowy veil of the Bride, and the whole right side of the cañon, are in deep shade, and its serried margin strongly relieved against the bright moonlit sky. On the other side are the cliffs of El Capitan, snow-white in the moonlight.

Above all arched the deep black sky, studded with stars gazing quietly downward. Here, under the black arching sky and before the grand cliffs of Yosemite, I lifted my heart in humble worship to the great God of *Nature*.

AUGUST 8.—Today we leave Yosemite; we therefore get up very early, intending to make an early start. I go out again into the meadow, to take a final farewell view of Yosemite. The sun is just rising; wonderful, warm, transparent golden light (like Bierstadt's picture) on El Capitan; the whole other side of the valley in deep, cool shade; the bald head of South Dome glistening in the distance. The scene is magnificent.

But see! just across the Merced River from our camp, a bare trickling of water from top to bottom of the perpendicular cliff. I have not thought it worth while to mention it before; but this is the fall called the *Virgin's Tears*. Poor Virgin! She seems *passée*, her cheeks are seamed and channeled and wrinkled; she wishes she was a Bride, too, and had a veil; so near El Capitan, too, but he will not look that way. I am sorry I have neglected to sing her praises.

We experienced some delay in getting off this morning. Our horses have feasted so long on this meadow that they seem disinclined to be caught. Pomroy's ill-favored beast, "Old 67," gave us much trouble. He had to be lassoed at last. We forded the river immediately at our camp. Found it so deep and rough that several of the horses stumbled and fell down. We now took Coulterville trail; up, up, up, backward and forward— up, up, up the almost perpendicular side of the cañon below the gate. The trail often runs on a narrow ledge, along the almost perpendicular cliff. A stumble might precipitate both horse and rider one thousand feet to the bottom of the chasm. But the horses know this as well as we. They are very careful. About the place where Mono trail turns sharp back from Coulterville trail, Mr. Muir overtook us. Without him we would have experienced considerable difficulty for the trail being now little used, except by shepherds, is very rough, and so blind that it is almost impossible to find it, or, having found, to keep it. My horse cast two of his shoes today.

Yet I had examined them before leaving Yosemite, and found them all right.

Made about fourteen miles, and about 2 P.M. reached a meadow near the top of Three Brothers. Here we camped for the night in a most beautiful grove of fir—*Abies concolor* and *magnifica*, chose our sleeping-places; cut branches of spruce and made the most delightful elastic and aromatic beds, and spread our blankets in preparation for night. After dinner, lay down on our blankets and gazed up through the magnificent tall spruces into the deep blue sky and the gathering masses of white clouds. Mr. Muir gazes and gazes, and cannot get his fill. He is a most passionate lover of nature. Plants and flowers and forests, and sky and clouds and mountains seem actually to haunt his imagination. He seems to revel in the freedom of this life. I think he would pine away in a city or in conventional life of any kind. He is really not only an intelligent man, as I saw at once, but a man of strong, earnest nature, and thoughtful, closely observing, and original mind. I have talked much with him today about the probable manner in which Yosemite was formed. He fully agrees with me that the peculiar cleavage of the rock is a most important point, which must not be left out of account. He further believes that the valley has been wholly formed by causes still in operation in the Sierra—that the Merced Glacier and the Merced River and its branches, when we take into consideration the peculiar cleavage, and also the rapidity with which the fallen and falling boulders from the cliffs are distintegrated into dust, have done the whole work. The perpendicularity is the result of cleavage; the want of talus is the result of the rapidity of disintegration and the recency of the disappearance of the glacier. I differ with him only in attributing far more to preglacial action. I may, I think, appropriately introduce here my observations on the evidence of glacial action in Yosemite.

It is well known that a glacier once came down the Tenaya Cañon. I will probably see abundant evidences of this high up this cañon tomorrow and next day. That this glacier extended into the Yosemite has been disputed, but is almost certain. Mr. Muir also tells me that at the top of Nevada Fall there are unmistakable evidences (polishings and scorings) of a glacier. There is no doubt, therefore, that anciently a glacier came down each of these cañons. Did they meet and form a Yosemite glacier? From the projecting rocky point which separates the Tenaya from Nevada Cañon, there is a pile of boulders and débris running out into the valley, near Lamon's garden, like a continuation of the point. Mr. Muir thinks this unmistakably a medial moraine, formed by the union of the Tenaya and Nevada glaciers. I did not examine it carefully. Again, there are two lakes in the lower Tenaya Cañon —viz., Mirror Lake and a smaller lake lower down. Below Mirror Lake, and again below the smaller lake, there is an immense heap of boulders and rubbish. Are not these piles formed by moraines, and have not the lakes been formed by the consequent damming of the waters of the Tenaya? These lakes are filling up. It seems probable that the meadow, also, on which we camped, has been formed in the same way, by a moraine just below the meadow, marked by a pile of débris there, also. Whether the succession of meadows in the Yosemite, of which the Bridal-veil Meadow is the lowest, have been similarly formed, requires and really deserves further investigation. I strongly incline to the belief that they have been, and that a glacier once filled Yosemite. I observed other evidences, but I must visit this valley again and examine more carefully.

After discussing these high questions with Mr. Muir for some time, we walked to the edge of the Yosemite chasm, and out on the projecting point of Three Brothers, called Eagle Point. Here we had our last, and certainly one of the most magnificent, views of the valley and the High Sierra. I can only name the points which are in view and leave the reader to fill out the picture. As we look up the valley, to the near left is the Yosemite Falls, but not a very good view; then Washington Column, North Dome; then grand old South Dome. The view of this grand feature of Yosemite is here magnificent. It is seen in half profile. Its rounded head, its perpendicular rock face, its towering height, and its massive proportions are well seen. As the eye travels round to the right, next comes the Nevada Fall (Vernal is not seen); then in succession the peaks on the opposite side of the valley—Glacier Point,

Sentinel Dome, Sentinel Rock, Cathedral Spires, and Cathedral Rock; then, crossing the valley, and behind us, is El Capitan. In the distance, the peaks of the Sierra—Mt. Hoffmann, Cathedral Peak, Clouds Rest, Mt. Starr King, Mt. Clark, and Ostrander's Rocks are seen. Below, the whole valley, like a green carpet, and Merced River, like a beautiful vine, winding through. We remained and enjoyed the view by sunlight, by twilight, and by moonlight. We then built a huge fire on the extreme summit. Instantly answering fires were built in almost every part of the valley. We shouted and received answer. We fired guns and pistols, and heard reports in return. I counted the time between flash and report, and found it nine to ten seconds. This would make the distance about two miles in an air-line.

About 8 P.M. went back to camp and supper, and immediately after to bed. During the night some of the horses, not having been staked, wandered away, and some of the party—Soulé, Hawkins, and Cobb—were out two hours recovering them. They found them several miles on their way back to the fat pasture of Bridalveil Meadow. My own horse had been securely staked. On my fragrant elastic bed of spruce boughs, and wrapped head and ears in my blankets, I knew nothing of all this until morning.

Coming out of the Yosemite today, Mr. Muir pointed out to me, and I examined, the Torreya. Fruit solitary, at extreme end of spray, nearly the color, shape, and size of a greengage plum, and yet a conifer. The morphology of the fruit would be interesting.

AUGUST 9.—Got up at daybreak this morning much refreshed. I am cook again today. My bread this morning was voted excellent. Indeed, it was as light and spongy as any bread I ever ate. About 12 M. we saw a shepherd's camp, and rode up in hopes of buying a sheep. No one at home; but there is much sheep-meat hanging about and drying. As we came nearer, a delicious fragrance assailed our nostrils, and set our salivaries in action. "A premonitory moistening overflowed my nether lip." What could it be? Here is a pot nearly buried in the hot ashes, and closely covered. Wonder what is in it. Let us see. On removing the cover a fragrant steam arose, which fairly overcame the scruples of several of the party. Mutton stew, deliciously seasoned! Mr. Muir, who, had been a shepherd himself, and had attended sheep here last year, and became thoroughly acquainted with shepherds' habits, assured us that we might eat without compunction—that the shepherd would be pleased rather than displeased—that they had more mutton than they knew what to do with. Upon this assurance we fell to, for we were very hungry, and the stew quickly disappeared. We all declared, and will always believe, that there never was such mutton stew made in this world before. While we were yet wiping our mustaches (such as had that ornament), the shepherd appeared, and was highly amused and pleased at our extravagant praises of his stew. Our appetites were, however, not yet half-appeased. We went on a little farther and stopped for noon at a small open meadow. While I was cooking dinner, Hawkins bought and butchered a fat sheep. There are thousands of sheep in this region. We expect to live upon mutton until we cross the Sierra.

This afternoon we went on to Lake Tenaya. The trail is very blind, in most places detectable only by the blazing of trees, and very rough. We traveled most of the way on a high ridge. When about two miles of our destination, from the brow of the mountain ridge upon which we had been traveling, Lake Tenaya burst upon our delighted vision, its placid surface set like a gem amongst magnificent mountains, the most conspicuous of which are Mt. Hoffmann group on the left, and Cathedral Peak beyond the lake. From this point we descended to the margin of the lake, and encamped at 5 P.M. on the lower end of the lake, in a fine grove of tamaracks, near an extensive and beautiful meadow. We built an immense fire, and had a fine supper of excellent bread and delicious mutton. Our appetites were excellent; we ate up entirely one hind-quarter of mutton and wanted more.

After supper, I went with Mr. Muir and sat on a high rock jutting into the lake. It was full moon. I never saw a more delightful scene. This little lake, one mile long and a half-mile wide, is actually embosomed in the mountains, being surrounded by rocky eminences two thousand feet

high, of the most picturesque forms, which come
down to the very water's edge. The deep stillness of the night; the silvery light and deep
shadows of the mountains; the reflection on the
water, broken into thousands of glittering points
by the ruffled surface; the gentle lapping of the
wavelets upon the rocky shore—all these seemed
exquisitely harmonized with one another and the
grand harmony made answering music in our
hearts. Gradually the lake surface became quiet
and mirror-like, and the exquisite surrounding
scenery was seen double. For an hour we remained
sitting in silent enjoyment of this delicious scene,
which we reluctantly left to go to bed. Tenaya
Lake is about eight thousand feet above sea-level.
The night air therefore is very cool.

I noticed in many places today, especially as we
approached Lake Tenaya, the polishings and
scorings of ancient glaciers. In many places we
found broad, flat masses so polished that our
horses could hardly maintain their footing in
passing over them. It is wonderful that in granite
so decomposable these old glacial surfaces should
remain as fresh as the day they were left by the
glacier. But if ever the polished surface scales off,
then the disintegration proceeds as usual. The
destruction of these surfaces by scaling is in
fact continually going on. Whitney thinks the
polished surface is hardened by pressure of the
glacier. I cannot think so. The smoothing, I think,
prevents the retention of water, and thus prevents the rotting. Like the rusting of iron, which is
hastened by roughness, and still more by rust,

and retarded, or even prevented, by cleaning and polishing, so rotting of rock is hastened by roughness, and still more by commencing to rot, and retarded or prevented by grinding down to the *sound* rock and then polishing.

Today, while cooking midday meal, the wind was high and the fire furious. I singed my whiskers and mustache and badly burned my hand with boiling-hot bacon fat.

AUGUST 10.—Early start this morning for Soda Springs and Mt. Dana. Phelps and his mare entertained us while getting off this morning with an amusing bucking scene. The interesting performance ended with the grand climacteric feat of flying head foremost over the head of the horse, turning a somersault in the air, and alighting safely on his back. After this exhilarating diversion, we proceeded on our way, following the trail on the right hand of the lake. Onward we go, in single file, I leading the pack over the roughest and most precipitous trail (if trail it can be called) I ever saw. At one moment we lean forward, holding to the horse's mane, until our noses are between the horse's ears; at the next, we stand in the stirrups, with our backs leaning hard against the roll of blankets behind the saddle.

Thus we pass, dividing our attention between the difficulties of the way and the magnificence of the scenery, until 12 M., when we reached Soda Springs, in the splendid meadows of the upper Tuolumne River.

Our trail this morning has been up the Tenaya Cañon, over the divide, and into the Tuolumne Valley. There is abundant evidence of an immense former glacier, coming from Mt. Dana and Mt. Lyell group, filling the Tuolumne Valley, overrunning the divide, and sending a branch down the Tenaya Cañon. The rocks in and about Tenaya Cañon are everywhere scored and polished. We had to dismount and lead over some of these polished surfaces. The horses' feet slipped and sprawled in every direction, but none fell. A conspicuous feature of the scenery on Lake Tenaya is a granite knob, eight hundred feet high, at the upper end of the lake and in the middle of the cañon. This knob is bare, destitute of vegetation, round and polished to the very top. It has evidently been enveloped in the icy mass, and its shape has been determined by it. We observed similar scorings and polishings on the sides of the cañon, to an equal and much greater height. Splendid view of the double peaks of the Cathedral, from the Tenaya Lake and from the trail. Looking back from the trail soon after leaving the lake, we saw a conspicuous and very picturesque peak, with a vast amphitheater, with precipitous sides, to the north, filled with a grand mass of snow, evidently the fountain of an ancient tributary of the Tenaya Glacier. We call this *Coliseum Peak*.* So let it be called hereafter, to the end of time.

* [Note in edition of 1900.] This sometimes called Tenaya Peak.

The Tuolumne Meadow is a beautiful grassy plain of great extent, thickly enameled with flowers, and surrounded with the most magnificent scenery. Conspicuous amongst the hundreds of peaks visible are Mt. Dana, with its grand symmetrical outline and purplish red color; Mt. Gibbs, of gray granite; Mt. Lyell and its group of peaks, upon which great masses of snow still lie; and the wonderfully picturesque group of sharp, inaccessible peaks (viz., Unicorn Peak, Cathedral Peaks, etc.), forming the Cathedral group.

Sode Springs is situated on the northern margin of the Tuolumne Meadow. It consists of several springs of ice-cold water, bubbling up from the top of a low reddish mound. Each spring itself issues from the top of a small subordinate mound. The mound consists of carbonate of lime, colored with iron deposited from the water. The water contains principally carbonates of lime and iron, dissolved in excess of carbonic acid, which escapes in large quantities, in bubbles. It possibly, also, contains carbonate of soda. It is very pungent, and delightful to the taste. Before dinner we took a swim in the ice-cold water of the Tuolumne River.

About 3 P.M. commenced saddling up, intending to go on to Mt. Dana. Heavy clouds have been gathering for some time past. Low mutterings of thunder have also been heard. But we had already been so accustomed to the same, without rain, in the Yosemite, that we thought nothing of it. We had already saddled, and some had mounted, when the storm burst upon us. "Our provisions—sugar, tea, salt, flour—must be kept dry!" shouted Hawkins. We hastily dismounted, constructed a sort of shed of blankets and india-rubber cloths, and threw our provisions under it. Now commenced peal after peal of thunder in an almost continuous roar, and floods of rain. We all crept under the temporary shed, but not before we had gotten pretty well soaked. So much delayed that we were now debating—after the rain—whether we had not better remain here overnight. Some were urgent for pushing on, others equally so for staying. Just at this juncture, when the debate ran high, a shout, "Hurrah!" turned all eyes in the same direction. Hawkins and Mr. Muir had scraped up the dry leaves underneath a huge prostrate tree, set fire and piled on fuel, and already, see!— a glorious blaze! This incident decided the question at once. With a shout, we ran for fuel, and piled on log after log, until the blaze rose twenty feet high. Before, shivering, crouching, and miserable; now joyous and gloriously happy.

The storm did not last more than an hour. After it, the sun came out and flooded all the landscape with liquid gold. I sat alone at some distance from the camp and watched the successive changes of the scene—first, the blazing sunlight flooding meadow and mountain; then the golden light on mountain peaks, and then the lengthening shadows on the valley; then a roseate bloom diffused over sky and air, over mountain and meadow. Oh, how exquisite! I never saw the like before. Last, the creeping shadow of night, descending and enveloping all.

The Tuolumne Meadows are celebrated for their fine pasturage. Some twelve to fifteen thousand sheep are now pastured here. They are divided into flocks of about twenty-five hundred to three thousand. I was greatly interested in watching the management of these flocks, each by means of a dog. The intelligence of the dog is perhaps nowhere more conspicuous.

The sheep we bought yesterday is entirely gone—eaten up in one day. We bought another here—a fine, large, fat one. In an hour it was butchered, quartered, and a portion on the fire, cooking. After a very hearty supper, we hung up our blankets about our camp-fire to dry, while we ourselves gathered around it to enjoy its delicious warmth. By request of the party, I gave a familiar lecture, or rather talk, on the subject of glaciers, and the glacial phenomena we had seen on the way.

LECTURE ON GLACIERS AND THE GLACIAL PHENOMENA OF THE SIERRA
[ABSTRACT]

In certain countries, where the mountains rise into the region of perpetual snow, and where other conditions, especially abundant moisture, are present, we find enormous masses of *ice* occupying the valleys, extending far below the snow-cap, and slowly moving downward. Such moving icy extensions of the perpetual snow-cap are called *glaciers*.

It is easy to see that both the existence of glaciers and their downward motion are necessary to satisfy the demands of the great universal *Law of Circulation*. For in countries where glaciers exist the amount of snow which falls on mountaintops is far greater than the waste of the same by melting and evaporation in the same region. The snow, therefore, would accumulate without limit if it did not move down to lower regions, where the excess is melted and returned again to the general circulation of meteoric waters.

In the Alps, glaciers are now found ten to fifteen miles long, one to three miles wide, and five hundred to six hundred feet thick. They often reach four thousand feet below the snow-level, and their rate of motion varies from a few inches to several feet per day. In grander mountains, such as the Himalayas and Andes, they are found of much greater size; while in Greenland and the Antarctic continent the whole surface of the country is completely covered, two thousand to three thousand feet deep, with an *ice sheet*, molding itself on the inequalities of surface, and moving slowly seaward, to break off there into masses which form icebergs. The *icy* instead of *snowy* condition of glaciers is the result of pressure, together with successive thawings and freezings. Snow is thus slowly compacted into *glacier-ice*.

Although glaciers are in continual motion downward, yet the lower end, or *foot*, never reaches below a certain point; and under unchanging conditions, this point remains fixed. The reason is obvious: The glacier may be regarded as being under the influence of two opposite forces; the downward motion tending ever to lengthen, and the melting tending ever to shorten it. High up the mountain the motion is in excess, but as the melting power of sun and air increases downward, there must be a place where the motion and the melting balance each other. At this point will be found the foot. It is called the lower limit of the glacier. Its position, of course, varies in different countries, and many even reach the seacoast, in which case icebergs are formed. *Annual* changes of temperature do not affect the position of the foot of the glacier, but *secular* changes cause it to *advance* or *retreat*. During periods of increasing cold and moisture the foot advances, pushing before it the accumulating débris. During periods of increasing heat and dryness it retreats, leaving its previously accumulated débris lower down the valley. But whether the *foot of the glacier* be stationary, or advancing or retreating, the matter of the glacier, and therefore all the débris lying on its surface, is in continual motion downward. Since glaciers are limited by melting, it is evident that a river springs from the foot of every glacier.

Moraines.—On the surface, and about the foot of glaciers, are always found immense piles of heterogeneous débris, consisting of rock fragments of all sizes, mixed with earth. These are called *moraines*. On the surface, the most usual form and place is a long heap, often twenty to fifty feet high, along each side, next the bounding cliffs. These are called *lateral moraines*. They are ruins of the crumbling cliffs on each side, drawn out into continuous line by the motion of the glacier. If glaciers are without tributaries, these lateral moraines are all the débris on their surface; but if glaciers have tributaries, then the *two* interior lateral moraines of the tributaries are carried down the middle of the glacier, as a *medial moraine*. There is a medial moraine for every tributary. In complicated glaciers, therefore, the whole surface may be nearly covered with débris.

All these materials, whether lateral or medial, are borne slowly onward by the motion of the glacier, and finally deposited at its foot, in the form of a huge, irregularly crescentic pile of débris known as the *terminal moraine*. If a glacier runs from a rocky gorge out on a level plain, then the lateral moraines may be dropped on either side, forming parallel débris piles, confining the glacier.

Laws of Glacial Motion.—Glaciers do not *slide* down their beds, like solid bodies, but *run* down in the manner of a body half-solid, half-liquid—i.e., in the manner of a *stream of stiffly viscous substance*. Thus, while a glacier slides over its bed, yet the upper layers move faster, and therefore slide over the lower layers. Again, while the whole mass moves down, rubbing on the bounding sides, yet the middle portions move faster, and therefore slide on the marginal portions. Lastly, while a glacier moves over *smaller* inequalities of bed and bank like a solid, yet it conforms to and molds itself upon the *larger* inequalities, like a liquid. Also, its motion down steep slopes is greater than over level reaches. Thus, glaciers, like rivers, have their *narrows* and their *lakes*, their rapids and their stiller portions, their *deeps* and their *shallows*. In a word, a glacier is a *stream*, its motion is *viscoid*, and, for the practical purposes of the geologist, it may be regarded as a very stiffly viscous body.

Glaciers as a Geological Agent.—Glaciers, like rivers, *wear away* the surfaces over which they pass; *transport* materials and *deposit* them in their course, or at their termination. But in all these respects the effects of glacial action are very characteristic, and cannot be mistaken for those of any other agent.

Erosion.—The cutting or wearing power of glaciers is very great; not only on account of their great weight, but also because they carry, fixed firmly in their lower surfaces, and therefore between themselves and their beds, rock fragments of all sizes, which act as their graving tools. These fragments are partly torn off from their rocky beds in their course, but principally consist of top-débris, which find their way to the bottom through fissures, or else are engulfed in the viscous mass on the sides. Armed with these graving tools, a glacier behaves toward smaller inequalities like a solid body, planing them down to a smooth surface, and marking the *smooth surface* thus made with *straight parallel scratches*. But to large inequalities it behaves like a viscous liquid, conforming to their surfaces, while it smooths and scratches them. It molds itself upon large prominences and scoops out large hollows, at the same time smoothing, rounding, and scoring them. These smooth, rounded, scored surfaces, and these scooped-out rock basins, are very characteristic of glacial action. We have passed over many such smooth surfaces this morning. The scooped-out rock basins, when left by the retreating glacier, become beautiful lakes. Lake Tenaya is probably such a lake.

Transportation.—The carrying power of river currents has a definite relation to velocity. To carry rock fragments, of many tons weight, requires an almost incredible velocity. Glaciers, on the contrary, carry on their surfaces, with equal ease, fragments of all sizes, even up to hundreds of tons weight. Again, boulders carried by water currents are always bruised and rounded, while glaciers carry them safely and lay them down in their original angular condition. Again, river currents always leave boulders in *secure* position, while glaciers may set them down gently, by the melting of the ice, in insecure positions, as *balanced stones*. Therefore, *large angular* boulders, different from the country rock, and especially if in *insecure* positions, are very characteristic of glacial action.

Deposit—Terminal Moraine. — As already seen, all materials accumulated on the surface of a glacier, or pushed along on the bed beneath,

Journal of Ramblings

find their final resting-place at the foot, and there form the *terminal moraine*. If a glacier recedes, it leaves its terminal moraine, and makes a new one at the new position of its foot. Terminal moraines, therefore, are very characteristic signs of the former position of a glacier foot. They are recognized by their irregular crescentic form, the mixed nature of their materials, and the entire want of stratification or sorting. Behind the terminal moraines of retired glaciers accumulate the waters of the river which flows from its foot, and thus again form lakes. Glacial lakes—i.e., lakes formed by the action of former glaciers—are therefore of two kinds—viz., (1) The filling of scooped-out rock basins; (2) the accumulation of water behind old terminal moraines. The first are found, usually, high up; the second, lower down the old glacial valleys.

Glacial Epoch in California.—It is by means of these signs that geologists have proved that at a period, very ancient in human but very recent in geological chronology, glaciers were greatly extended in regions where they still exist, and existed in great numbers and size in regions where they no longer exist. This period is called the *Glacial Epoch*. Now, during this glacial epoch, the whole of the High Sierra region was covered with an ice-mantle, from which ran great glacial streams far down the slopes on either side. We have already seen evidences of some of these ancient glaciers on *this*, the western, slope. After crossing Mono Pass, we will doubtless see evidences of those which occupied the eastern slope.

In our ride yesterday and today, we crossed the track of some of these ancient glaciers. From where we now sit, we can follow with the eye their pathways. A great glacier (the Tuolumne Glacier) once filled this beautiful meadow, and its icy flood covered the spot where we now sit. It was fed by several tributaries. One from Mt. Lyell, another from Mono Pass, and still another from Mount Dana, which uniting just above Soda Springs, the swollen stream enveloped yonder granite knobs five hundred feet high standing directly in its path, smoothing and rounding them on every side, and leaving them in form like a turtle's back; then coming farther down overflowed its banks at the lowest point of yonder ridge—one thousand feet high—which we crossed this morning, and after sending an overflow stream down Tenaya Cañon the main stream passed on down the Tuolumne Cañon into and beyond Hetch Hetchy Valley. From its head fountain, in Mt. Lyell, this glacier may be traced forty miles.

The overflow branch which passed down the Tenaya Cañon, after gathering tributaries from the region of Cathedral Peaks, and enveloping, smoothing, and rounding the grand granite knobs which we saw this morning just above Lake Tenaya, scooped out that lake basin, and swept on its way to the Yosemite. There it united with other streams from Little Yosemite and Nevada cañons, and from Illilouette, to form the great Yosemite Glacier, which probably filled that valley to the brim and passed on down the cañon of the Merced. This glacier, in its subsequent retreat, left many imperfect terminal moraines, which are still detectable as rough débris piles, just below the meadows. Behind these moraines accumulated water, forming lakes, which have gradually filled up and formed meadows. Some, as Mirror Lake, have not yet filled up. The meadows of Yosemite, and the lakes and meadows of Tenaya Fork, upon which our horses grazed while we were at University Camp, were formed in this way. You must have observed that these lakes and meadows are separated by higher ground, composed of coarse débris. All the lakes and meadows of this High Sierra region were formed in this way. The region of good grazing is also the region of former glaciers.

Erosion in High Sierra Region.—The erosion to which this whole High Sierra region had been subjected in geological times is something almost incredible. It is a common popular notion that mountain peaks are *upheaved*. No one can look about him observantly in this High Sierra region and retain such a notion. Every peak and valley now within our view, all that constitutes the grand scenery upon which we now look, is the result wholly of erosion—of *mountain sculpture*. Mountain chains are indeed formed by igneous agency; but these are afterwards sculptured into forms of beauty. But even this gives as yet no adequate idea of the immensity of this erosion; not only are all the grand peaks now within view—Cathedral Peaks, Unicorn Peak,

Mt. Lyell, Mt. Gibbs, Mt. Dana—the result of simple inequality of erosion; but it is almost certain that the slates which form the foothills, and over whose upturned edges we passed, from Snelling to Clark's, and whose edges we again see, forming the highest crests on the very margin of the eastern slope, originally covered the granite of this whole region many thousand feet deep. Erosion has removed it entirely, and bitten deep into the underlying granite. Now, you are not to imagine that the whole, but certainly a large portion, of this erosion, and the final touches of this sculpturing, have been accomplished by the glacial action which we have endeavored to explain.

About 9 P.M., our clothing still damp, we rolled ourselves in our damp blankets, lay upon the still wet ground, and went to sleep. I slept well and suffered no inconvenience.

To any one wishing really to enjoy camp-life in the High Sierra, I know no place more delightful than Soda Springs. Being about nine thousand feet above the sea, the air is deliciously cool and bracing. The water, whether of the spring or of the river, is almost ice-cold, and the former a gentle tonic. The scenery is nowhere more glorious. Add to this, inexhaustible pasturage for horses and plenty of mutton, and what more can pleasure seekers want?

AUGUST 11.—As we intended going only to the foot of Mt. Dana, a distance of about eleven miles, we did not hurry this morning. The mutton gotten yesterday must be securely packed; we did not get started until 9 A.M. Trail very blind. Lost it a dozen times, and had to scatter to find it each time. Saw again this morning magnificent evidences of the Tuolumne Glacier. Among the most remarkable several smooth, rounded knobs of granite, eight hundred to one thousand feet high, with long slope up the valley, and steep slope down the valley, evidently their whole form determined by an enveloping glacier.

About 2 P.M., as we were looking out for a camping-ground, a thunder-storm again burst upon us. We hurried on, searching among the huge boulders (probably glacial boulders) to find a place of shelter for our provisions and ourselves. At last we found a huge boulder which overhung on one side, leaning against a large tree. The roaring of the coming storm grows louder and louder, the pattering of rain already commences. "Quick! quick!!" In a few seconds the pack was unsaddled and provisions thrown under shelter. Then rolls of blankets quickly thrown after them; then the horses unsaddled and tied; then, at last, we ourselves, though already wet, crowded under. It was an interesting and somewhat amusing sight. All our provisions and blanket rolls and eleven men packed away, actually piled upon one another, under a rock which did not project more than two and a half feet. I wish I could draw a picture of the scene: the huge rock with its dark recess; the living, squirming mass, piled confusedly beneath; the magnificent forest of grand trees; the black clouds; the constant gleams of lightning, revealing the scarcely visible faces; the peals of thunder, and the floods of rain, pouring from the rock on the projecting feet and knees of those whose legs were inconveniently long, or even on the heads and backs of some who were less favored in position.

In about an hour the storm passed, then sun again came out, and we selected camp. Beneath a huge prostrate tree we soon started a fire, and piled log upon log, until the flame, leaping upward, seemed determined to overtop the huge pines around. Ah, what joy is a huge camp-fire! —not only its delicious warmth to one wet with rain in this high cool region, but its cheerful light, its joyous crackling and cracking, its frantic dancing and leaping! How the heart warms and brightens and rejoices and leaps in concert with the camp-fire!

We are here nearly ten thousand feet above sea-level. Our appetites are ravenous. We eat up a sheep in a day; a sack (one hundred pounds) of flour lasts us five or six days. Nights are so cool that we are compelled to make huge fires, and sleep near the fire to keep warm.

Our camp here is a most delightful one, in the midst of grand trees and huge boulders—a meadow hard by, of course, for our horses. By stepping into the meadow, we see looming up very near us on the south the grand form of Mt. Gibbs, and on the north the still grander form of Mt. Dana. After supper and dishwashing and horse-tending and fire-replenishing the young men gathered around me, and I gave them the following:

LECTURE ON DEPOSITS IN CARBONATE SPRINGS

You saw yesterday and this morning the bubbles of gas which rise in such abundance to the surface of Soda Springs. You observed the pleasant pungent taste of the water, and you have doubtless associated both of these with the presence of carbonic acid. But there is another fact which probably you have not associated with the presence of this gas—viz., the *deposit of a reddish substance*. This reddish substance, which forms the mound from the top of which the spring bubbles, is carbonate of lime, colored with iron oxide. This deposit is very common in carbonated springs. I wish to explain it to you.

Remember, then, first, that lime carbonate and metallic carbonates are insoluble in pure water, but slightly soluble in water containing carbonic acid; second, that the amount of carbonates taken up by water is proportionate to the amount of carbonic acid in solution; third, that the amount of carbonic acid which may be taken in solution is proportioned to the pressure. Now, all spring water contains a small quanity of carbonic acid, derived from the air, and will therefore dissolve limestone (carbonate of lime); but the quantity taken up by such waters is so small that it will not deposit except by drying. Such are not called carbonated springs.

But there are also *subterranean* sources of carbonic acid, especially in volcanic districts. Now, if percolating water come in contact with such carbonic acid—being under heavy pressure—it takes up larger quantities of the gas. If such waters come to the surface, the pressure being removed, the gas escapes in bubbles. This is a carbonated spring.

If, further, the subterranean water thus highly charged with carbonic acid comes in contact with limestone or rocks of any kind containing carbonate of lime, it dissolves a proportionately large amount of this carbonate, and when it comes to the surface the escape of the carbonic acid causes the limestone to deposit, and hence this material accumulates immediately about the spring and in the course of the stream issuing from the spring.

The kind of material depends upon the manner of deposit and upon the presence or absence of iron. If the deposit is tumultuous, the material is *spongy*, or even pulverulent; if quiet, it is *dense*. If no iron be present, the deposit is white as marble; but if iron be present, its oxidation will color the deposit yellow, or brown, or reddish. If the amount of iron be variable, the stone formed will be beautifully striped. Suisun marble is an example of a beautifully striped stone, deposited in this way in a former geological epoch.

I have said that such springs are most common in volcanic districts. They are therefore commonly warm. Soda Springs, however, is not in a volcanic district. In our travels in the volcanic region on the other side of the Sierra, we will find, probably, several others. At one time these springs were far more abundant in California than they are now.

AUGUST 12.—We had cooked bread yesterday for our breakfast and lunch today, in anticipation of our ascent of Mt. Dana. We had this morning only to cook meat. This takes but little time. We made an early start, therefore. Rode our horses up as far as the timber extends, staked them out in little green patches of rich grass, very abundant on the mountain slopes, and then commenced the real ascent on foot. I think we ascended about three thousand feet after leaving our horses. Saw a splendid buck—but alas! Cobb has left his rifle. Mt. Dana, as seen from this side, is of a very regular conical form, entirely destitute of soil, and therefore of vegetation; in fact, from top to bottom, a mere loose mass of rock fragments—metamorphic sandstone and slates. The slope is, I think, forty degrees; the rock fragments, where small, give way under the foot and roll downward; if large, they are difficult to climb over. The ascent is difficult and fatiguing in the extreme. The danger, too, to those below, from boulders loosened by the feet of those above, is very great. A large fragment, at least one hundred pounds, thus loosened by Mr. Bolton, came thundering down upon me with fearful velocity before I was aware. I had no time to get out of the way; in fact, my own footing was precarious. I opened my legs; it passed between and bounded on its way down.

There being no trail, each man took his own way. The young men were evidently striving to see who could be up first. I took my steady, even way, resting a moment from time to time. My progress illustrated the fable of the hare and tortoise. I was the third man on the top. Mr. Muir and Pomroy alone had gotten there before me. I really expected to find the whole party there.

The view from the top is magnificent beyond description. To the southwest, the sharp, strangely picturesque peaks of the Cathedral group. To the south, in the distance, Mt. Lyell group, with broad patches of snow on their slopes; and near at hand, the bare gray mass of Mt. Gibbs. To the north, the fine outline of Castle Peak, rising above and dominating the surrounding summits; and to the east, almost at our feet, the whole interior valley, including Lake Mono, with its picturesque islands and volcanoes. Stretching away to the west, valleys with grassy meadows and lakes separated by low wooded ridges. I could count thirty to fifty of these lakes, and meadows without number. These meadows and lakes and ridges suggest glacier beds, with moraines, stretching westward down the Sierra slope.

As already stated, the whole mountain is superficially a mass of loose rock fragments. I saw the rock *in situ* only in one place, but this was a magnificent section. About two-thirds way up, the bed-rock appears as a perpendicular crag, nearly one hundred feet high. It is here a very distinctly and beautifully stratified sandstone, and is a perfectly *horizontal* position. The slope on the western and southwestern side is regular and about forty degrees, but when we arrived on the top we found that on the east and northeast the slope is very precipitous, forming an immense amphitheater, in which lay immense stores of snow, and in one place we found nestled a clear, deep-blue lake, apparently formed by the melting snow. This great snow-field extends a little over the gentle slope by which we ascended. For the last five hundred to one thousand feet we ascended the mountain over this snow. Mt. Dana is 13,227 feet high. I did not observe any remarkable effect of diminlished density of atmosphere upon respiration or circulation. The beating of the heart was a little troublesome. I had to stop frequently to allow it to become quiet; but this seemed to me as bad or worse near the beginning of the climb than near the top. It seemed only more difficult than usual to get my "second wind," as it is called. We took cold lunch on the top of the mountain and commenced our descent, which was less fatiguing, but much more dangerous and trying than the ascent. The shoes of several of the party were completely destroyed. Mine still hold out. Came back to camp at 2 P.M., tired but not exhausted. Soon after reaching camp, we again had thunder and rain. We all huddled with our provisions and blankets again under our rock shed. There was but a sprinkle this time, however, though much threatening of wind and thunder.

After supper we again built up an immense camp-fire. Now, while I write, the strong light of the blazing camp-fire is thrown upon the tall tamarack trees, and upon the faces of the young men, engaged in various ways. I wish I could draw a picture of the scene now presented: the blazing fire of huge piled logs; the strongly illuminated figures of the party; the intense blackness of sky and forest. Supper is just over. Mr. Stone is squatting on the ground, engaged in washing up dishes. Mr. Linderman, who is cook today, is lying on his back, kicking up his heels, and regarding Mr. Stone with intense satisfaction. His work is over, while Stone's is just begun. Mr. Muir is earnestly engaged hollowing out a place under a huge pine tree, which he intends to make his resting-place for the night. Captain is lying down flat on his back, with his clasped hands under his head and his eyes closed. Pomroy is sitting in the strong light of the fire, writing his journal; he is this moment scratching his cropped poll for an idea. Bolton, Phelps, and Perkins are sitting together near the fire, Bolton enjoying his cigarette, and Phelps and Perkins chatting. Cobb is just returning with another log for the fire. Hawkins has been looking after his horse and is just returning. I am observing the scene and jotting down these crude notes.

We will see Mono Lake tomorrow. Before going to bed, therefore, the party gathered about the fire, and by request I gave them the following lecture on the formation of salt and alkaline lakes.

LECTURE ON SALT AND ALKALINE LAKES

Salt Lakes may originate in two general ways: either by the isolation of a portion of sea water, or else by the indefinite concentration of ordinary river water in a lake without an outlet. The Great Salt Lake and all the other salt lakes scattered over the desert on the other side of the Sierra are possibly formed by the first method. It is probable that at a comparatively recent geological epoch the whole of the salt and alkaline region on the other side of the Sierra, which we will see tomorrow, was covered by an extension of the sea from the Gulf of California. When this was raised into land, portions of sea water were caught up and isolated in the hollows of the uneven surface. The lakes thus formed have since greatly diminished by drying away, as is clearly shown by the terraces, or old water levels, far beyond and above the present limits; and their waters have become saturated solutions of the saline matters contained in sea water.*

The Dead Sea, and many other salt lakes and

---

* [Note in edition of 1900.] More recent observations render it almost certain that Great Salt Lake and other lakes in the basin region were formed by the concentration of river water. Some of these lakes (e.g., Pyramid Lake, Walker Lake, etc.) are much fresher than sea water. (December, 1899.)

brine pools in the interior of Asia, have probably been formed in the same way. But the Caspian Sea is probably an example of the second method of formation; i.e., by concentration of river water. The reason for thinking so is, that old beach marks, or terraces, show a great drying away of the lake, and yet the water is still far less salt than sea water.

Alkaline lakes are formed, and can be formed, only by the second method; viz., by indefinite concentration of river water by evaporation in a lake without an outlet. Such concentration, therefore, may form either a salt or an alkaline lake. Whether the one or the other kind of lake results, depends wholly upon the composition of the river water. If chlorides predominate, the lake will be salt; but if alkaline carbonates predominate, it will be alkaline.

Perhaps some of you will be surprised that the pure fresh water of mountain streams can produce salt or alkaline lakes. I must therefore try to explain.

We speak of spring water as pure and fresh; it is so comparatively. Nevertheless, all spring water, and therefore all river water, contains small quantities of saline matters derived from the rocks and soils through which they percolate. Suppose, then, the drainage of any hydrographical basin to accumulate in a lake. Suppose, further, that the *supply* of water by rivers be greater than the *waste* by evaporation from the lake surface. It is evident that the lake will rise, and, if the same relation continues, it will continue to rise until it finds an outlet in the lowest part of the rim, and is discharged into the ocean or some other reservoir. Such a lake will be *fresh*, i.e., it will contain only an imperceptible quantity of saline matter.

But if, on the other hand, at any times the *waste* by evaporation from the lake surface should be equal to the supply by rivers, the lake would not rise, and therefore would not find an outlet. Now the salting process will commence. The waters which flow in contain a little, be it ever so little, of saline matter. All this remains in the lake, since evaporation carries off only distilled water. Thus, age after age saline matters are leached from rocks and soils, and accumulated in the lake, which, therefore, must eventually become either salt or alkaline.

Thus, whether lakes are saline or fresh depends on the presence or absence of an outlet, and the presence or absence of an outlet depends on the relation of supply by rain to waste by evaporation, and this latter depends on the climate. Saline lakes cannot occur except in very dry climates, and these lakes are rare, because on most land surfaces the rainfall far exceeds the evaporation, the excess being carried to the sea by rivers. Only in wide plains, in the interior of continents, do we find the climatic conditions necessary to produce salt lakes.

I have shown the conditions necessary to the formation of a salt lake by concentration of river water. Now, the very same conditions control the existence of salt lakes, however they may have originated. Even in the case of a salt lake formed by the isolation of a portion of sea water, whether it remain salt or become fresh will depend wholly on the conditions discussed above.

Suppose, for example, a portion of sea water be isolated by an upheaval of the sea-bed; now, if the supply of water to this lake by rivers be greater than the waste by evaporation from the surface, the lake will rise, overflow, and discharge into the sea or other reservoir; the salt water will be slowly rinsed out, and the lake will become fresh. But if the evaporation should equal the supply, the lake will not find an outlet, and will remain salt, and will even increase in saltness until it begins to deposit.

Thus, if the Bay of San Francisco should be cut off from the sea at the Golden Gate, it would form a fresh lake, for the water running into it by the Sacramento River is far greater than the evaporation from the bay. So the Black Sea, and the Baltic Sea, as above shown by the comparative freshness of the waters, would form fresh lakes. But the Mediterranean, as shown by the great saltness of its waters, would certainly remain salt, and become increasingly salt. We have the best reasons to believe that Lake Champlain, since the glacial epoch, was an arm of the sea. It has become fresh since it became separated.

Saltness of the Ocean.—Thus, then, we see that the one condition which determines the existence of salt and alkaline lakes is the absence of an outlet. Now, the ocean, of course, has no outlet; the ocean is the final reservoir of saline matters leached from the earth. Hence, although the saltness of the ocean is a somewhat different problem from that of salt lakes, yet it is almost certain that the saline matters of the ocean are the accumulated results of the leachings of the rocks and soils by circulating waters throughout all geological times.

During my travels through the Sierra I have made many observations on rocks and mountains. One or two of these I think worthy of mention. First, I have seen everywhere the strongest confirmation of the view that granite and granitic rocks may be but the final term of metamorphism of sedimentary rocks. In Yosemite I could trace every stage of gradation from granite into gneiss, and, since leaving Yosemite, from gneiss into impure sandstones. On Mt. Dana sandstones are easily traced into gneiss, or even eurite, and slate into a crystalline rock, undistinguishable from diorite or other traps.

Second, no one who examines the forms of the peaks of the Sierra can come to any other conclusion than that all the mountain forms seen here are the result of *erosion*. Standing at Soda Springs and gazing upon the strange forms of the Cathedral group, the conviction is forced upon the mind that these were not upheaved, but simply left as more resisting fragments of an almost inconceivable erosion—fragments of a denuded plateau. The strange ruggedness of the forms, the inaccessible peaks and pinnacles, have been the result of the very decomposable nature of the granite. Mt. Dana, with its more regular form, consists of more resistant slates. The evidence that Mt. Dana has been formed entirely by erosion is, I conceive, complete. As already stated, Mt. Dana is composed of un-distributed horizontal strata. The grand bulge of a great mountain chain is probably produced by the shrinkage of the earth; the folding and tiltings of strata in mountain chains by the same cause; but the actual forms which constitute scenery are purely the result of aqueous erosion. Metamorphism is, I believe, always produced in deeply buried rocks by heat, water, and pressure. The universal metamorphism of the rocks in the Sierra is therefore additional evidence of the immensity of the erosion which brings these to the surface.

Since leaving Yosemite we have seen no houses; in fact, no human beings but a few shepherds. As the flocks require to be driven from one pasture to another, these men live only in hastily constructed sheds, covered with boughs. In this shepherd's life there may be something pleasant when viewed through the imagination only; but in reality it is enough to produce either imbecil-ity or insanity. The pleasant pictures drawn by the poets, of contemplative wisdom and harm-less enjoyment, of affectionate care of the flock, of pensive music of pipes—these possibly, prob-ably, once did exist; but certainly they do not exist now, at least in California.

August 13.—Cold last night. We had to sleep near the fire, and keep it up during the night. Considerable frost this morning, for we are in the midst of the snows. We got up early, feeling bright and joyous, and enjoyed our breakfast as only mountaineers can. Over Mono Pass, and down Bloody Cañon today. I really dread it, for my horse's sake. Even well-shod horses get their feet and legs cut and bleeding in going down this cañon. My horse, since leaving Yosemite, has lost three shoes, and has already become very tender-footed. Got off by 6 A.M. Sorry, very sorry, to leave our delightful camp here. In commemoration of the delightful time we have spent here, we name it "Camp Dana."

The trail to the summit is a very gentle ascent, the whole way along the margin of a stream. Distance, three or four miles. Saw a deer, but Cobb was not on hand. On the very summit, 10,700 feet high, there is a marshy meadow, from which a stream runs each way: one east, into the Tuolumne, along which we had ascended; the other west, down Bloody Cañon into Mono Lake, along which we expect to descend. Right on the summit, and in Bloody Cañon, we found great masses of snow. The trail passes by their edges and over their surfaces. The trail down Bloody Cañon is rough and precipitous beyond conception. It is the terror of all drovers and packers across the mountains. It descends four thousand feet in two or three miles, and is a mere mass of loose fragments of sharp slate. Our horses' legs were all cut and bleeding before we got down. I really felt pity for my horse, with his tender feet. We all dismounted and led them down with the greatest care. In going down we met a large party of Indians, some on horseback, and some on foot, coming up. We saluted them. In return they invariably whined, "Gie me towaca," "Gie me towaca." They were evidently incredulous when told that none of the party chewed.

The scenery of Bloody Cañon is really magnificent, and, in a scientific point of view, this is the most interesting locality I have yet seen. Conceive a narrow, winding gorge, with black slaty precipices of every conceivable form, fifteen hundred to two thousand feet high on either side. As the gorge descends precipitously, and winds from side to side, we often look from above down into the most glorious amphitheater of cliffs, and from time to time beyond, upon the glistening surface of Lake Mono, and the boundless plains, studded with volcanic cones. About one-third way down, in the center of the grandest of these amphitheaters, see! a deep, splendidly clear emerald-green lake, three or four times the size of Mirror Lake. It looks like an artificial basin, for its shores are everywhere hard, smooth, polished rock; especially the rim at the lower side is highly polished and finely striated. There can be no doubt that this lake basin has been scooped out by a glacier which once descended this cañon. In fact, glacial action is seen on every side around this lake, and all the way down the cañon and far into the plains below.

The cliffs on each side are scored and polished to the height of one thousand feet or more; projecting knobs in the bottom of the cañon are rounded and scored and polished in a similar manner.

After we had descended the steep slope, and had fairly escaped from the high rocky walls of Bloody Cañon proper; after we had reached the level plain and had prepared ourselves for an extensive view, we found ourselves still confined between two huge parallel ridges of débris five hundred feet high and only half a mile apart, and extending five or six miles out on the plain.

There are the *lateral moraines* of a glacier which once descended far into the plain toward Mono Lake. A little below the commencement of these moraines, in descending, we found a large and beautiful lake filling the whole cañon. Below this lake the lateral moraines on either side send each a branch which meet each other, forming a crescentic cross-ridge through which the stream breaks. This is evidently a *terminal* moraine, and the lake has been formed by the damming up of the water of the stream by this moraine barrier.

Below this, or still farther on the plain, I observed several other terminal moraines, formed in a similar way, by curving branches from the lateral moraines. Behind these are no lakes, but only marshes and meadows. These meadows are evidently formed in the same way as the lake; in fact, were lakes, subsequently filled up by deposit.

After getting from these lateral moraines fairly out on the plains, the most conspicuous objects which strike the eye are the extinct volcanoes. There are, I should think, at least twenty of them, with cones and craters as perfect as if they erupted yesterday. Even at this distance, I see that their snow-white, bare sides are composed of loose volcanic ashes and sand, above which projects a distinct rocky crater-rim, some of dark rock, but most of them of light-colored, probably pumice rock. Magnificent views of these cones and of Mono Lake are gotten from time to time, while descending Bloody Cañon. The cones are of all heights, from two hundred to twenty-seven hundred feet above the plain, and the plain itself about five thousand feet above sea-level.

We stopped for lunch at a cabin and meadow —a cattle ranch—about five miles from the lake. While our horses grazed, we cooked our dinner as usual, and then proceeded three miles and camped in a fine meadow on the banks of a beautiful stream—Rush Creek.

In riding down to our camp, I observed the terraces of Lake Mono, former water-levels, very distinctly marked, four or five in number. The whole region about Lake Mono, on this side, is covered with volcanic ashes and sand. It is the only soil except in the meadows. Even these seem to have the same soil, only more damp, and therefore more fertile. Scattered about, larger masses of pumice and obsidian are visible. Except in the meadows and along streams, the only growth is the sagebrush. Just before reaching camp, Mr. Muir and myself examined a fine section, made by Rush Creek, of lake and river deposit, beautifully stratified. It consists below of volcanic ashes, carried as sediment and deposited in the lake, and is therefore a true lake deposit, and beautifully stratified. Above this is is a drift pebble deposit; the pebbles consisting of granite and slate from the Sierra. Above this again, are volcanic ashes and sand, *unstratified*, probably blown ashes and sand, or else ejected since the drift. We have therefore certain evidence of eruptions before the drift, and possibly, also, after.

In the picture of the view from Mono Lake, I have yet said nothing about the Sierra. The general view of the range from this, the Mono, side is far finer than from the other side. The Sierra rises gradually on the western side for fifty or sixty miles. On the Mono, or eastern, side it is precipitous, the very summit of the range running close to the valley. From this side, therefore, the mountains present a sheer elevation of six or seven thousand feet above the plain. The sunset view of the Sierra, from an eminence near our camp, this evening, was, it seems to me, by far the finest mountain view I have ever in my life seen. The immense height of the chain above the plain, the abruptness of the declivity, the infinitely diversified forms, and the wonderful sharpness and ruggedness of the peaks, such as I have seen nowhere but in the Sierra, and all this strongly relieved against the brilliant sunset sky, formed a picture of indescribable grandeur. As I turn around in the opposite direction, the regular forms of the volcanoes, the placid surface of Lake Mono, with its picturesque islands, and far away in the distance the scarcely visible outlines of the White Mountains, pass in succession before the eye. I enjoyed this magnificent panoramic view until it faded away in the darkness.

From this feast I went immediately to another, consisting of excellent bread and such delicious mutton chops! If any restaurant in San Francisco could furnish such, I am sure it would quickly make a fortune. Some sentimentalists seem to think that these two feasts are incompatible; that the enjoyment of the beautiful is inconsistent with voracious appetite for mutton. I do not find it so.

After supper I again went out to enjoy the scene by night. As I gazed upon the abrupt slope of the Sierra, rising like a wall before me, I tried to picture to myself the condition of things during the glacial epoch. The long western slope of the Sierra is now occupied by long, complicated valleys, broad and full of meadows, while the eastern slope is deeply graven with short, narrow, steep ravines. During glacial times, therefore, it is evident that the western slope was occupied by long, complicated glaciers, with comparatively sluggish current; while on the east, short, simple parallel ice-streams ran down the steep slope and far out on the level plain. On each side of these protruded icy tongues: the débris brought down from the rocky ravines was dropped as parallel moraines. Down the track of one of these glaciers, and between the outstretched *moraine arms*, our path lay this morning.

AUGUST 14 (SUNDAY).—I have not before suffered so much from cold as last night; yet yesterday the sun was very hot. No grand forests to protect us from wind and furnish us with logs for camp-fire; only sagebrush on the plains and small willows on the stream-banks. The winds blow furiously from the Sierra down the cañons upon the plains. Got up at 4 A.M.; couldn't sleep any more. After breakfast, went to visit the volcanic cones in the vicinity.* The one we visited was one of the most perfect, and at the same time one of the most accessible. It was not more than one hundred and fifty or two hundred feet above the level of the sandy plain on which it stands.

I was very greatly interested in this volcano. It seems to me that its structure clearly reveals some points of its history. It consists of two very perfect cones and craters, one within the other. The outer cone, which rises directly from the

---

* While on the way, had a very fine view, toward the east, of the terraces of Lake Mono. I think there must be five or six very perfect.

level plain to a height of two hundred feet, is composed wholly of volcanic sand, and is about one mile in diameter. From the bottom and center of its crater rises another and much smaller cone of lava to a little greater height. We rode up the outer sand cone, then around on the rim of its crater, then down its inner slope to the bottom; tied our horses to sagebrush at the base of the inner lava cone, and scrambled on foot into its crater. Standing on the rim of this inner crater, the outer rises like a rampart on every side.

I believe we have here a beautiful example of cone-and-rampart structure, so common in volcanoes elsewhere; the rampart, or outer cone, being the result of an older and much greater eruption, within the wide yawning crater, of which by subsequent lesser eruption the smaller cone was built.*

Mr. Muir is disposed to explain it differently. He thinks that this was once a much higher single cone, lava at top and sand on the slopes, like most of the larger cones in this vicinity; and that after its last eruption it suffered *engulfment* —i.e., its upper rocky portion has dropped down into its lower sandy portion.

The lava of this volocano is mostly pumice and obsidian, sometimes approaching trachyte. It was of all shades of color, from black to white,

---

* I again in 1875 visited this region. My observations on several of the volcanoes confirmed my first impressions.

sometimes beautifully veined, like slags of an iron furnace; and of all physical conditions, sometimes vesicular, sometimes glassy, sometimes stony. Wrinkled fusion-surfaces were also abundant. Again, I believe I can fix the date of the last eruption of this volcano. I found on the outer cone (or ash cone) several unmistakable drift *pebbles of granite.* At first I thought they might be the result of accidental deposit; but I found, also, several within the *lava crater.* These were reddened and semi-fused by heat. There can be no doubt, therefore, that the last eruption of this volcano was since the drift; it broke through a layer of drift deposit, and threw out the drift pebbles. Some fell back into the crater.

Mr. Muir took leave of us within the crater of this volcano. He goes today to visit some of the loftier cones. I would gladly accompany him, but my burnt hand has today become inflamed, and is very painful. The climb of twenty-seven hundred feet, over loose, very loose sand, will be very fatiguing, and the sun is very hot. In spite of all this, I had determined to go; but the party are impatient of delays.

I was really sorry to lose Mr. Muir from our party. I have formed a very high opinion of, and even a strong attachment for, him. He promises to write me if he observes any additional facts of importance.

We came back to camp about 12 M., and while dinner was preparing, took a delightful swim in the river which runs here by our camp into the lake. Several Indians visited us while at dinner. This is a favorite time for such visits. They know they will get something to eat. Two younger Indians were full of life and good-nature, but one old wrinkled fellow was very reticent, and stood much upon his dignity. He had a beautiful bow and several arrows. We put up some bread and the younger ones shot for it; but the old Indian would take no notice of it, and even seemed to treat the idea with contempt. He evidently belongs to the "Old Régime." He remembers the time when the *noble* red man had undisputed possession of this part of the country.

About 2 P.M. we started for Alliton's, a small house on the west side of the lake, and about twelve miles distant. Here I hope to have my horse temporarily shod. In this hope I have picked up and preserved three horseshoes. If we can find nails at Alliton's, Hawkins will shoe my horse. If not, I know not what I shall do, for my horse is so lame he can hardly get on at all today. Had it not been for the lameness of my horse, I would have enjoyed the evening ride greatly. The trail runs close along the margin of the lake, sometimes in the very water, sometimes rising on the slopes of the steep mountains, which come down to the very water's edge. From the sides of these mountains the view of the lake and mountains was very fine. The volcanic character of the islands in the lake was very evident, and their craters were quite distinct. It is said that evidences of feeble volcanic activity still exist in the form of steam-jets, hot springs, etc. I am anxious to visit these islands, and will do so if I can. My horse was so lame that I made very slow progress, and lagged behind several miles. When I reached Alliton's I found the house empty—Alliton not at home, and the party gone to a house about a mile or two farther on. Alas! what shall I do for my horse? Soon after leaving Alliton's, however, I met Hawkins, riding Cobb's pony bareback. He said he had found some shoenails at Alliton's, and he would shoe my horse. We therefore exchanged horses; I went on, and he back to Alliton's, and shod my horse very nicely.

On my way along the shores of the lake I observed thousands of birds—blackbirds, gulls, ducks, magpies, stilts, sandpipers. The sandpipers I never saw alight on the shore, but only on the water. They swam, rose in flocks, settled on the water exactly like true ducks.* Will not these in time undergo a Darwinian change into web-footers? These birds seem to collect in such numbers to feed upon the swarms of flies which frequent the shores. The number of these is incredible. I saw them in piles three or four inches thick on the water, and in equal piles thrown up dead on the shore. The air stank with them. These flies come here to spawn. Their innum-

---

* [Note in edition of 1900.] These, I afterward learned, are not true sandpipers, but *Phalaropes*, and are indeed partially web-footed.

erable larvæ form, I understand, the principal
food of the Indians during a portion of the year.*
All about the margin of the lake, and standing
in the water near the shore, I observed irregular
masses of rough, porous limestone, evidently deposited from the water of the lake, or else from
limestone springs.

Soon after camping we went in swimming in
the lake. The water is very buoyant, but the
bathing is not pleasant. The shores are flat and
muddy, and swarm with flies. These do not
trouble one, but their appearance is repulsive.
The water contains large quantities of carbonate
of soda, a little carbonate of lime, and probably
some borax. It therefore is very cleansing, but
makes the skin feel slimy, and lathers the head
and beard like soap. The presence of volcanic
rocks and volcanic sand all around, and also of
soda granite in the Sierra, sufficiently explains
why this lake is alkaline instead of salt.

We bought here a little butter, cheese, and
corned beef, and enjoyed them very much for
supper. We have gotten out of the region of
mutton. With the exception of patches of rich
meadow, formed by the streams from the Sierra,
everywhere is sage, sage, sage! The water, however, is delicious. The streams are formed by the
melting snows of the Sierra, and these are so near

---

*I have since (1875) observed the gathering of the
larvæ, or rather pupæ, of these flies. About the 1st of July
the pupæ are cast ashore in immense quantities. They are
then gathered, dried, rubbed to break off the shell, and
kept for use under the name of *Koo-chah-bee*.

by that the water is very abundant and ice-cold. Close by our camp there issues from a large rough limestone rock a magnificent spring of ice-cold water which runs off as a large brook.

Most of our party concluded to sleep here in a hayloft. Hawkins and myself preferred a haycock. We put our blankets together, and had a deliciously soft, warm, and fragrant bed, under the starlit sky.

I desired very much to visit the islands from this point, but there was no boat. These islands, I understand, are the resort of millions of gulls, which deposit their eggs there in immense quantities. These eggs are an important article of food and of traffic for the Indians. Mono Lake is about fifteen miles long and twelve miles across.

AUGUST 15.—Got up at 4:30 A.M., greatly refreshed by a fine night's rest. Got off about 7 A.M., in fine spirits. My horse is nearly well of his lameness this morning. Soon after leaving our camp this morning, we passed a rude Indian village, consisting of a few huts. The Indian huts in this region are nothing but a few poles, set up together in a conical form and covered with boughs. We bought from these Indians several quarts of pine-nuts.* They are about the size and nearly the shape of ground-pea kernels. We found them very sweet and nice. On leaving Mono we struck out nearly northwest. We were

* Nut of the *Pinus monophylla*.

therefore soon amongst the foothills of the Sierra again, and consequently in the mining regions. Saw many evidences of superficial mining. The débris of these washings by the whites are washed over by the Chinese. Passed quite a village of Chinese engaged in this way. The diminutive mud huts were strung along a little stream—Virginia Creek—in the bottom of a ravine, for a considerable distance. The whites call this Dog Town. I observed, even here, almost every hut had its little irrigated garden-patch attached to it. I had an opportunity, also, of examining the process of hydraulic mining by the whites, and was much interested.

About 11 A.M. we met a fruit-wagon loaded with fruit and other supplies, which had come over Sonora Pass, and was on its way to Mono. With a loud yell, the whole party made a simultaneous dash for the wagon, clambered up its sides, and swarmed over the boxes. Peaches, grapes, apples! Ah, how we enjoyed these delicious luxuries!

After making about twenty miles this morning, we camped for noon, about 12:30 P.M., at Big Meadows. This is a beautiful grassy plain, six or seven miles long and three or four miles wide, on which graze hundreds of cattle and horses. The view from this plain is superb. Now, as I sit here at our noon camp, I am surrounded on every side by mountains. Behind me, to the east, are the foot-hills we have just crossed; in front stretches the green meadow, and beyond rises the lofty Sierra.

The nearer mountains are immense, somewhat regular masses, smooth and green to the very summits, except where covered with patches of snow. Behind these, and seen through gaps, are the most magnificent group of singularly sharp and jagged peaks, tinged with blue by their distance, with great masses of snow in the deep hollows on their precipitous faces. The appearance of these great amphitheaters, with precipitous walls, suggested at once that these were the wombs from which once issued great glaciers. I wish my dear friends in Oakland could see us now—some eating, some washing up, some playing ball, some lolling about, and our saddles and packs grouped together where we unsaddled, our horses grazing quietly on the green meadow, and the whole surrounded by this really magnificent mountain scenery.

This afternoon we are wanting some supplies. Some of the party are sadly in want of shoes; some of the horses need shoeing. While three of the party, Captain, Pomroy, and Bolton, go to Bridgeport, a small town on Big Meadows—distinctly visible from our camp, and but little out of our way—the main body of the party went straight on, intending to choose camp and make fire before the rest came. Started about 4 P.M., intending to go only about seven miles and then camp in a cañon which we see emerging into Big Meadows, on the northwest—"Tamarack Cañon." As the sun went down behind the Sierra, the view became more and more splendid, and the coolness of the evening air increased our enjoyment of it. The delight of that evening ride, and the glory of that mountain view, I shall never forget.

About 6:30 found a place in the cañon where the grazing was very fine and water abundant—the grass and clover fresh, tall, and juicy, and a little stream gurgling close by. Here we camped, turned our horses loose to graze, with lariats trailing, intending to stake them securely before going to bed. In the meantime it became very dark, and our companions not yet arrived. We made a rousing fire, and waited, hungry and impatient. They had the pack and the supplies. When at last they did arrive, which was about 9 P.M., they came shouting and yelling and hurrahing at the sight of the blazing fire. The noise stampeded our horses, and they ran affrighted and snorting up the steep sides of the cañon, over the mountains, and away into the impenetrable darkness of night. We could trace them only by their shrill snorting, and now and then by the flitting form of my old gray. After some fruitless attempts to recover them, which only increased their fright, the night being very dark and the mountains very rough, we concluded to give it up until morning, and went to bed feeling much uneasiness.

We have been today on the first road we have seen since we left Clark's.

AUGUST 16.—At daybreak, two of the party, Hawkins and Linderman, went after the horses. By the time breakfast was ready they returned with them. They had tracked them over the mountains back to Big Meadows, where they found them quietly feasting, about three miles from camp. We started off about 8 A.M., and for eight or ten miles more traveled on the Sonora road, along the same narrow cañon in which we had camped. This cañon is not more than one hundred yards wide, flanked on each side by very steep hills and precipices, yet the bottom is quite level and the road good. Passed immense masses of trap—ancient lava flows. In some places they are finely columnar. Mostly porphyritic lava and amygdaloid.

About ten miles from our camp, we reached Warm Springs. These are very fine and very large springs. A considerable brook runs directly from the principal spring. There are, moreover, several springs, having different properties. The waters seem to be violently boiling, but this is the result of escaping carbonic acid rather than steam. The temperature of the water seems to be about 150 to 160 degrees. Everything suitable for a watering-place is found here—hot baths, vapor baths, accommodations for visitors, etc.,—although in somewhat rude style. We have here still another evidence of the decay of the mines in this region. This was once a flourishing watering-place, or at least expected to become so; but it is now entirely abandoned. Several parties are now stopping here to make use of the baths, and to hunt and fish in the vicinity. They bring, of course, their own provisions. Sage-hens are very abundant in the brush, and trout in the streams, in this region. I observe limestone now depositing from these carbonated springs. Also, near by, immense rough masses of the same, which have been similarly deposited at some previous epoch. The immense laval streams in this immediate vicinity, in fact all around, sufficiently account for the heat of these springs.

After examining the springs we rode on, leaving the Sonora road and taking a trail for Antelope Valley. Rain now coming on, we galloped on until we came to a good grazing meadow, about three miles from the Warm Springs. There was here a rude pole house—probably a shepherd's lodge—which sufficiently protected us and our provisions from the rain. Here, therefore, we camped for noon. While here, a party of ladies and gentlemen rode by and camped a little beyond. They had a wagon for protection. The ladies seemed to be true Amazons—managed their horses with the utmost ease, dashed about in the most fearless manner, saddled and unsaddled, mounted and dismounted, without assistance. They were, in short, true cavaliers in petticoats.

This afternoon, the rain detained us here a little longer than we had intended. Started about 3:30 P.M. Delightful ride in the cool of the evening. All in high spirits. We reached a ridge overlooking Antelope Valley about sunset. Before us Antelope Valley lay spread out at our feet (but ah! how far below us we found to our cost that night), behind us the magnificent Sierra, and the sun setting behind it. We stopped and gazed first at one and then at the other.

"Antelope Valley is but a step; what is the use of hurrying?"

"Nevertheless, we had better go on. Remember Laddsville and Chowchilla Mountain."

On we rode. Presently a cañon, right across the way—and such a cañon!

"Surely it is impossible to cross that!"

A thousand feet deep, and less than a thousand feet wide at the top, and the sides seemingly perpendicular! But across it we must go. Already we see Hawkins and the advanced guard near the top on the other side. We speak to them across the yawning chasm. The trail wound backward and forward, down one side, across the foaming stream, and then backward and forward up the other side. We followed the trail, though it led us on the dizzy edge of fearful precipices. We have become accustomed to this sort of thing, and so have our horses.

Onward we pushed; next across an inextricable tangle of sagebrush and trap boulders; then down another cañon, and across another ridge; then down, down, down; then over another ridge, and darkness overtook us. Then down, down, down! We lost the trail; scattered about to find it. "Here it is!"—found again; lost again; scatter; found again, and so on; but always still down, down, down! At last we reached the plain after descending at least four thousand feet. In the valley at last! But alas! no meadow; nothing but sage, sage, sage! Very dark; neither moon nor stars. Onward we push, guided only by lights we see in the valley. "Hello! where are you?" we hear from behind. "Here! come on!" we answered. We stop a while until laggers come up. Onward again we urge our tired horses, winding through the sagebrush. Onward, still onward, straining our eyes to peer through the thick darkness. Onward, still onward, five long miles, through the interminable sage desert, without trail, and guided only by the lights. One by one the lights disappear. "What shall we do? Can't stop here. Push on." At last reached some Indian huts.

"How far to white man's house?"

"Leetle ways."

"How many miles?"

"No savé."

"One mile?—two mile?—half mile?"

"No savé."

Onward, still onward! In despair we stopped to consult. At the Indian huts we had struck a road; but it was leading us away from the direction in which we had seen the lights. We again struck into the pathless sage. Hawkins is reconnoitering, a little in advance. "Here we are!" we heard him cry "Whoop! A barley field!" It was without a fence. We determined to ride in, unsaddle, make our camp, allow our horses to eat their fill of standing barley, and make it good by paying in the morning. It was 10 P.M. Some of the party were so tired and sleepy that they preferred to go to bed supperless, and therefore immediately threw themselves on the ground and went to sleep. Five of us, however, determined to build a fire and cook supper. Ah! what a glorious fire sagebrush makes! Ah, what a splendid supper we cooked that night! Ah, how we laughed in our sleeves at the mistake that the sleepers had made! Comforted and happy, and gazing complacently yet compassionately on the prostrate forms of our companions, moaning in their sleep with the pangs of hunger, we went to bed at 11:30 P.M. and slept sweetly the sleep of innocence. If we are trespassing, it is time enough to think of that in the morning.

We have ridden twenty-eight to thirty miles today, and about the same yesterday. Today the trail has been very rough. Our horses are quite tired.

AUGUST 17.—Woke up much refreshed by a sound, dreamless sleep. This valley can't be more than three to four thousand feet high. Last night was the warmest we have felt since we left Yosemite. I had just waked up. I was sitting on my blankets, putting on my shoes, and thinking repentantly of our trespass. The sun was just rising. Yonder comes swift retribution in the shape of a tall, rough-looking mountaineer, with rifle on shoulder and pistol in belt, galloping straight toward us. As he comes nearer, he looks pale, and his lips are firmly compressed. He stops before me suddenly.

"You seem to have had a good thing here last night?"

"Why, yes rather—but we intend, of course, to pay for it."

"I am glad to hear it."

He was evidently greatly provoked by our trespass, but after we had explained the circumstances, and had paid him four dollars, he seemed very well satisfied, bade us good-morning, put spurs to his horse, and rode off as rapidly as he had come.

We did not get off so early as usual this morning. The supperless ones slept heavily this morning and got up growling. Hawkins was up and out shooting by daybreak, and returned with a fine rabbit, which, with other camp delicacies, put all in good humor at breakfast.

Started about 8 o'clock. This valley being so deep, of course we had to climb very high to get out of it. The road is, however, tolerably good. We nooned about ten miles from Antelope Valley, at Silver King, a deserted mining town. This is a good example of many similar towns in the mining districts of California. They are rapidly built up—property rising to fabulous price—then as rapidly decay. This one seems to have flashed up and gone out more suddenly than usual. There are several rather pretentious but unfinished buildings—hotels, stores, etc. The lots are all staked out, and a few years ago were held at high prices. Evidences of mining operations close by. I examined these, but saw no evidence of any special value. We took possession of the hotel; used the barroom as our dining-room, and the bar-counter as our table. Made a hearty dinner, the young men all the while playing hotel life, laughing and calling "Waitaw! roast beef! Waitaw! bottle of champagne!" etc.

Three P.M.—Rode rapidly this evening, a good part of the way at an easy lope, and camped at a meadow in Bagsley's Valley, about two miles from Monitor. Here we found, to our great delight, a flock of sheep. We bought one and enjoyed mutton chops for supper again. After supper we all gathered around the campfire, and I gave the party a talk on the subjects of Bloody Cañon and its glacier, the volcanoes of Mono, and the lava flows and warm carbonated springs we saw yesterday; but as the substance of what I then said is scattered about among these notes, I omit it here.

It being quite cool tonight, Hawkins and myself concluded to bunk together.

AUGUST 18.—Last night was the coldest we have yet felt. Could not sleep very well for the cold. This morning, when I woke up, my blanket, hair, and beard were covered with a heavy frost. The meadow was white with the same. The water left overnight in our tin canister was frozen. A blazing fire, and plenty of mutton chops, bread, and hot tea soon thawed us, and by the time the sun was up an hour or so it was quite warm again. One of the shoes put on my horse by Mr. Hawkins, at Alliton's, being very thin at the point, has broken, and half of it come off. I found, on leaving camp this morning, that my horse was painfully lame again. The sharp fragments of rock which cover the road here make him shrink and limp and groan at every step. Fortunately the town of Monitor is only two miles off. I determined here to get him well shod all around. I stopped at Monitor for this purpose, while the rest of the party rode on to Markleeville, about eight miles farther, where they would stop, in order to get supplies for the party. While he was shoeing my horse, I sat and talked much with the blacksmith. I delight in seeing any work well done. He was master of his trade. I also delight in seeing a fine physique. He was a well-made, strong, and really handsome man. He was also a man of a few words and much good sense. I would like to meet that man again; I often think of him. I wonder if he has thought a second time of *me*? Probably not.

After shoeing, I hurried on and overtook the party at Markleeville. Here it was inconvenient to cook our own meal; so we all took dinner at the hotel. The dinner was really excellent, and we all enjoyed it greatly. Think of it! Besides the meats, which we could have had as good in camp, rice, in genuine Southern style (my heart warmed toward mine host), potatoes, beans, corn, pies, cakes, and sweetmeats. The variety tempted too much.

I received more letters from home at this place. Every one at home has been perfectly well since I left. I am light-hearted today. I shall be at home in a week or ten days. I wrote to that effect.

All along the road from Monitor to Markleeville, and in Markleeville itself, I have seen sad evidences of the effects of the speculative spirit— sad evidences of time and money and energies wasted. Deserted houses and deserted mines in every direction. The Indians, of whom there are a large number about Markleeville, occupy these deserted houses. Some of the mines which I saw seemed to have been undertaken on an expensive scale. They are mostly quartz-mines.

By invitation of Mr. Hawkins, we went on this afternoon only three miles, and camped at a ranch belonging to his brother. Beautiful ranch, nice meadows for our horses, rich butter and milk for ourselves, baths, hot, cold, and warm, issuing from fine springs. The place has been rudely fitted up for bathing.

This is indeed a most delightful place, and the party seem to feel its effects upon their spirits. While the horses graze, and I sit in the shade and write this, the young men are playing ball on the smooth-shaven green. The meadow is surrounded by high, almost perpendicular and apparently impassible mountains on every side except that by which we came. In such a secluded, beautiful dell, deep sunk in the mountaintop, might a Rasselas dream away his early life. Over those apparently impassable cliffs must we climb tomorrow, if we would go on to Tahoe. Hawkins had intended leaving us here, as he lives in this vicinity; but he has kindly volunteered to lead us over the mountains into Hope Valley, from which the road onward to Tahoe is very good.

I took here a hot bath, so hot I could hardly bear it, and immediately after an ice-cold shower. The effect was delightful. Most of the party slept here in a hay-loft. I preferred sleeping with Hawkins, in the open air, on a haystack.

AUGUST 19.—Heavy frost again this morning. Water and milk left from supper last night frozen. Took again, early this morning, the hot bath and cold shower. Mr. Hawkins observed yesterday for the first time that his horse is badly foundered. He takes another horse here, and by preference a powerful young horse, upon which man never sat before. Think of going over the most terrible mountain trail on such a horse! But he is accounted, I find, the best rider and horse-tamer in the county. He mounted his horse just before we were ready to start, and in half an hour he had tamed him completely.

The trail from this place into Hope Valley is one of the steepest we have yet attempted. It is a zigzag, up an almost perpendicular cliff. In many places there can be no doubt that a false step would have been certainly fatal to man and horse. In the steepest parts we dismounted and led the horses a great portion of the way up. In many places there was no detectable trail at all. When once up, however, the trail was very good. From the top of this ridge I saw many fine peaks of columnar basalt, evidently the remnants of old lava streams. The descent into Hope Valley is much more gentle. This valley is a famous resort for fishing and hunting parties. As we entered the valley, and were about to stop for noon, we met one of these—a large party of ladies and gentlemen. Of course, we straightened up and dashed by in fine style, and immediately dismounted and camped on a grassy meadow on the banks of the creek. They seemed much amused and somewhat astonished at our wild appearance.

Two P.M.—After resting here two hours, we started on our way to Tahoe. Here Hawkins left us. Every one of the party was sincerely affected. He has been the soul of our party. I don't believe we could have gotten along without him—so generous, so efficient, so thoroughly acquainted with camp and mountain life. He scents out a trail with the instinct of a bloodhound. As he turned, we all waved our hats and cried, "Three cheers for our noble Lieutenant! Hurrah! hurrah!! hurrah!!!" His face flushed and eyes filled. I know he was gratified with the heartiness of the salute.

We now proceeded by a good wagon-road, and therefore quite rapidly. About 5 P.M. rode in double file up to Yank's and reined up.* The fat, bluff old fellow cries out:

"Hello! where are you fellows from? Where are you going?"

"Excursion party to Tahoe; where best to stop?"

---

* [Note in editino of 1900.] Yank, some years after this, moved his hotel to the border of the lake.

"You want to have a free, jolly time, don't you?"

"O, yes, certainly."

"Well, you camp at this end of the lake, near Rowlands."

On we went, at a good round pace, and camped at 7 P.M. in a fine grove of tamaracks on the very borders of the lake.

We have, I observed this evening, passed through the region of slate (mining region) and the region of lava-flows, and are again in the region of granite. The granite about Tahoe. however, is finer-grained than that about Yosemite and Tuolumne Meadows, especially the latter.

AUGUST 20.—I am cook today. I therefore got up at daybreak and prepared breakfast while the rest enjoyed their morning snooze. After breakfast we hired a sail-boat, partly to fish, but mainly to enjoy a sail on this beautiful lake.

Oh, the exquisite beauty of this lake!—its clear waters, emerald-green, and the deepest ultramarine blue; its pure shores, rocky or cleanest gravel, so clean that the chafing of the waves does not stain in the least the bright clearness of the waters; the high granite mountains, with serried peaks, which stand close around its very shore to guard its crystal purity—this lake, not *among*, but *on*, the mountains, lifted six thousand feet towards the deep-blue overarching sky, whose image it reflects! We tried to fish for

trout, but partly because the speed of the sail-
boat could not be controlled, and partly because
we enjoyed the scene far more than the fishing,
we were unsuccessful, and soon gave it up. We
sailed some six or eight miles, and landed in a
beautiful cove on the Nevada side. Shall we go
in swimming? Newspapers in San Francisco say
there is something peculiar in the waters of this
high mountain lake. It is so light, they say, that
logs of timber sink immediately, and bodies of
drowned animals never rise; that it is impossible
to swim in it; that, essaying to do so, many good
swimmers have been drowned. These facts are
well attested by newspaper scientists, and therefore not doubted by newspaper readers. Since
leaving Oakland, I have been often asked by the
young men the scientific explanation of so sing-
ular a fact. I have uniformly answered, "We will
try scientific experiments when we arrive there."
That time had come.

"Now then, boys," I cried, "for the scientific
experiment I promised you!" I immediately
plunged in head foremost and struck out boldly.
I then threw myself on my back, and lay on
the surface with my limbs extended and motionless for ten minutes, breathing quietly the while.
All the good swimmers quickly followed. It is
as easy to swim and float in this as in any other
water. Lightness from diminished atmospheric
pressure! Nonsense! In an almost incompressible
liquid like water, the diminished density produced by diminished pressure would be more

than counterbalanced by increased density produced by cold.

After our swim, we again launched the boat and sailed out into the very middle of the lake. The wind had become very high and the waves quite formidable. We shipped wave after wave, so that those of us who were sitting in the bows got drenched. It was very exciting. The wind became still higher; several of the party got very sick, and two of them *cascaded*. I was not in the least affected, but, on the contrary, enjoyed the sail very much. About 2 P.M. we concluded it was time to return, and therefore tacked about for camp.

The wind was now dead ahead, and blowing very hard. The boat was a very bad sailer, and so perhaps were *we*. We beat up against the wind a long time and made but little headway. Finally, having concluded we would save time and patience by doing so, we ran ashore on the beach about a mile from camp and towed the boat home. The owner of the boat told us that *he* would not have risked the boat or his life in the middle of the lake on such a day. "Where ignorance is bliss," etc.

After a hearty supper, we gathered around the fire, and the young men sang in chorus until bedtime. "Now then, boys," cried I, "for a huge camp-fire, for it will be cold tonight!" We all scattered in the woods, and every man returned with a log, and soon the leaping blaze seemed to overtop the pines. We all lay around, with our feet to the fire, and soon sank into deep sleep.

AUGUST 21 (SUNDAY.)—Sunday at Tahoe! I wish I could spend it in perfect quiet. But my underclothes must be changed. Cleanliness is a Sunday duty. Some washing is necessary. Some of the party went fishing today. The rest of us remained in camp and mended or washed clothes.

At 12 M. I went out alone and sat on the shore of the lake, with the waves breaking at my feet. How brightly emerald-green the waters near the shore, and how deeply and purely blue in the distance! The line of demarcation is very distinct, showing that the bottom drops off suddenly. How distinct the mountains and cliffs all around the lake; only lightly tinged with blue on the farther side, though more than twenty miles distant!

How greatly is one's sense of beauty affected by associations! Lake Mono is surrounded by much grander and more varied mountain scenery than this; its waters are also very clear, and it has the advantage of several picturesque islands; but the dead volcanoes, the wastes of volcanic sand and ashes covered only by interminable sagebrush, the bitter, alkaline, dead, slimy waters, in which nothing but worms live; the insects and flies which swarm on its surface, and which are thrown upon its shore in such quantities as to infect the air—all these produce a sense of desolation and death which is painful; it destroys entirely the beauty of the lake itself; it unconsciously mingles with and alloys the pure enjoyment of the incomparable mountain scenery in its vicinity. On the contrary, the deep-blue pure waters of Lake Tahoe, rivaling in purity and blueness the sky itself; its clear, bright emerald shore waters, breaking snow-white on its clean rock and gravel shores; the lake basin, not on a plain, with mountain scenery in the distance, but countersunk in the mountain's top itself—these produce a never-ceasing and ever-increasing sense of joy, which naturally grows into love. There would seem to be no beauty except as associated with human life and connected with a sense of fitness for human happiness. Natural beauty is but the type of spiritual beauty.

Enjoyed a very refreshing swim in the lake this afternoon. The water is much less cold than that of Lake Tenaya or the Tuolumne River, or even the Nevada River.

The party which went out fishing returned with a very large trout. It was delicious.

I observe on the lake ducks, gulls, terns, etc., and about it many sandhill cranes—the white species. The clanging cry of these sounds pleasant to me by early association.

August 22.—Nothing to do today. Would be glad to sail on the lake or fish, but too expensive hiring boats. Our funds are nearly exhausted. Would be glad to start for home, but one of our party—Pomroy—has gone to Carson City, and we must wait for him. I went down alone to the lake; sat down on the shore and enjoyed the scene. Nothing to do, my thoughts today naturally went to the dear ones at home. Oh, how

I wish they could be here and enjoy with me this lovely lake! I could dream away my life here with those I love. How delicious a dream! Of all the places I have yet seen, this is the one which I could longest enjoy and love the most. Reclining thus in the shade, on the clean white sand, the waves rippling at my feet with thoughts of Lake Tahoe and of my loved ones mingling in my mind, I fell into a delicious doze. After my doze I returned to camp, to dinner.

About 5 P.M. took another and last swim in the lake.

Pomroy, who went to Carson, returned at 7 P.M. After supper, again singing in chorus, and then the glorious camp-fire.

AUGUST 23.—We all got up very early this morning. We wish to make an early start. All in high spirits; for we start for home today. I wonder if any one is half so anxious and impatient as I am. We wish to make Sacramento in three days. The distance is 110 miles or more. We must start early and ride late, if necessary. After camping three days in the same place, however, there is always much to collect and to fix. In spite of our early rising, we did not get off until about 7 A.M. Our route lay over Johnson Pass and by Placerville. We rode rapidly, however, alternately walking and galloping, and made twenty miles by 12 o'clock. About ten miles from Tahoe we reached the summit. We turned about here, and took our last look at the glorious lake, set like a gem in the mountains.

From the summit we rode rapidly down the splendid cañon of the south fork of the American River, here but a small brook, and stopped for noon about two miles below Strawberry, on a little grassy patch on the hillside, "close by a softly murmuring stream." Here we staked our horses, cooked and ate dinner, and "lolled and dreamed" for three hours, and then again saddled up and away.

Every pleasure has its pain, and every rose its thorn. We are in the region of good roads again —but oh, the dust! It is awful! About 4 P.M. saw a wagon coming; our instincts told us that it was a fruit-wagon. With a yell, we rushed furiously upon the bewildered old wagoner. "I surrender! I surrender!" he cried, while, with a broad grin, he handed out fruit and filled our extended hats. "A-a-ah! Peaches! grapes! apples!" How delicious on this hot, dusty road! Rode this evening eleven or twelve miles, the cañon becoming finer as we advanced, until, at Sugarloaf Gorge, it reaches almost Yosemite grandeur. Camped at 6 P.M. near an inn called "Sugarloaf," on account of a remarkable rock, several hundred feet high, close by. Our campfire was not far from the inn. At a window we saw two young ladies giggling and making merry at our cook—Mr. Linderman—mixing dough and baking bread. We sent them a piece, just to show them what we could do. No good ground to sleep on here. We don't relish sleeping in the dustry road. We therefore took our blankets and slept in the hay-loft. Although we left the window open, we found it rather close. Alas! alas! no more grand forests, no more grassy meadows, no more huge leaping camp-fires; only dusty roads, dirty villages, and stable lofts and stalls.

I have been observing the cañon down which we came today. Johnson Pass, like Mono Pass, was a glacial divide. One glacier went down on the Tahoe side, a tributary to the Tahoe Glacier, but a much larger glacier came down the American Cañon. Sugarloaf Rock has been enveloped and smoothed by it. This great glacier may be traced for twenty-five miles.

AUGUST 24.—As we got into the region of civilization again, incidents are less numerous. I observed, both yesterday and today, very many deserted houses. This was the Overland stage-road. Two years ago the amount of travel here was immense. I think I heard that there were twelve to fifteen stages a day. Now the travel is small, the railroad, of course, taking the travelers. The road is, however, splendidly graded, but the toll is heavy. This morning the road ran all the way along the American River, sometimes near the water's edge, but mostly high up the sides of the great precipitous cañon formed by the erosive power of the river. The scenery all the way yesterday and today is fine, but especially along the American River it is really very fine. If we had not already drunk so deep of mountain glory, we would call it magnificent. Again, this morning, walking and galloping alternately, we made easily twenty miles by 12 o'clock. Stopped for noon at "Sportsman's Hall," a roadside inn. Here, after dinner, we sold "Old Pack" for twenty dollars, exactly what we gave for him, left our cooking utensils (our supplies were just exhausted), and determined hereafter to take our meals at the inns on the roadsides or in the villages. Disencumbered of our pack, we could ride more rapidly.

This afternoon we rode sixteen miles: thirteen to Placerville, then through Placerville and three miles beyond, to Diamond Springs. On approaching Placerville, I observed magnificent orchards, cultivated by irrigation. I never saw finer fruit. Saw everywhere about and in Placerville abundant evidences of placer mining. The streams are also extensively used for this purpose, and are therefore all of them very muddy. Placerville is by far the largest and most thriving village I have seen since leaving Oakland. It probably contains two or three thousand inhabitants. The houses are stuck about along the streams and on the hillsides in the most disorderly manner, their position being determined neither by regularity nor beauty nor picturesque effect, but chiefly by convenience in mining operations. The streets are very few, very long, very irregular, very narrow. Nevertheless, the general effect is somewhat picturesque. As we rode into town, and passed in double file through the streets, Captain at the head, erect, and evidently feeling his dignity, the young men descried a billiard-saloon, became suddenly demoralized, broke ranks, incontinently dismounted, frantically rushed in, and immediately the click of the billiard-balls was heard. Greatly disgusted at such insubordination, the Captain rode on with me to the post-office. Here I mailed a letter to my wife, saying I would be at home probably on the night of the 26th. Onward then through the town for nearly a mile (it stretches so far along the stream), then up the hill, turned on the top and took a look at the town, pleasantly nestled below, among the hills; then over the toll-bridge and onward until, about dark, we reached the little village of Diamond Springs, and put up our horses at Siesbuttel's inn. Here we got as good a supper as any one could desire —and such coffee!

That night, to any attentive listener there must have been much good music in the stable—nine horses, crunching, crunching, below, and nine sleepers, snoring, snoring, above.

I was surprised to learn from our host that Placerville and vicinity is very sickly. Everybody suffering from chills and fever. He himself is suffering from this disease. Cause seems to be the stirring up of the earth by mining, and especially the damming up of waters for irrigation.

AUGUST 25.—Early start this morning. Got fairly off by 6 A.M. Rode rapidly, and made twenty-one miles by 11:30 A.M. Stopped for noon at the Halfway House. Took a swim—our very last —in a pond near by, and our dinner at the inn. Slept an hour, lying on the floor of the piazza;

rested our horses until 3 P.M., and then again onward for home.

In the afternoon we rode fourteen miles, to Patterson's Ten-mile House. We found this a delightful place. Mr. Patterson is really a very pleasant and courteous gentleman, and gave us a most excellent supper. This put us all in excellent humor. The young men got lively. One of them, Mr. Perkins, played on the piano, while the rest joined in a stag-dance. The clattering of heavy boots on the bare floor was not very harmonious, it is true, but then it was very enlivening. The host and all the guests in the house seemed to enjoy it hugely.

Two nights past we have been compelled to sleep in the stable loft, or else in the dusty streets. We are more fortunate tonight. There is a magnificent strawbank in the open field on the other side of the road. "Once more under the starry canopy! Now for a good sleep! Our Father up there in the starry heavens, watch over us. Amen!"

We are again on the plains of Sacramento, but we no longer find the heat oppressive. We have been all along the road mistaken for horse or cattle drovers, or for emigrants just across the plains. We were often greeted with, "Where's your drove?" or "How long across the plains?" We have been in camp nearly six weeks, and ridden five or six hundred miles. Burned skin, dusty hair and clothes, flannel shirt, breeches torn, and coarse, heavy boots—the mistake is quite natural.

AUGUST 26.—"Home today! Hurrah! Wake up, all!" After an early breakfast, got off 6:30 A.M. We rode into Sacramento, ten miles, in one and half hours, galloping nearly the whole way. We went at a good gallop in the regular order— double file—through the streets of Sacramento, whole length of the city, down to the wharf, and there tied our horses. Everybody crowded around, especially the little boys about the wharf, curious to know "who and what were these in strange attire."

Having nothing to do until 12 M., when the boat leaves, Captain and myself strolled through town. The Captain, with flannel shirt, bare neck, shocking bad hat, stout brogans, long knife stuck in belt, and a certain erect, devil-may-care air, certainly looked like a somewhat dangerous character. As we sauntered along the streets, a little sharp-looking Jew suddenly rushed out from his store, crying:

"Now, gentlemen, I know you are in want of clothes. Here we are,—the cheapest and finest in town. This way, gentlemen; this way!"

"No; we don't want any clothes; we have plenty at home."

"Aren't you the party who went galloping down the street just now?"

"Yes."

"Where are you from?"

"Only a pleasure party."

"Why, I thought you were outlaws, or cattle-drovers, or horse-dealers, or emigrants over the plains, or something of that kind."

We then visited the State House. As we walked along the corridors toward the well-dressed and courteous usher, the Captain looked very grand. The usher seemed instinctively to know that we were not exactly what we seemed. He treated us very courteously, and showed us the fine halls of Representatives and Senate.

We read, *cum ore rotundo*, the Latin inscriptions, and translated, to the great astonishment of the usher. We now went back to the wharf, and cut and ate cantaloupes; then to a restaurant, and had a most delicious dinner, of which we partook very heartily; then on board of the boat for San Francisco, and tied our horses all in a row and gave them hay! Then up into the cabin.

Everybody looked at us with interest and surprise. "Who are they?" Gradually it became known who we were, and we were treated with courtesy, and even became lions.

Captain of the boat took some of us up to his room and asked many questions. Dinner at 4 P.M. I went down, and again ate one of the heartiest dinners I ever ate in my life. I cannot get enough today.

Our rough appearance gave rise to some amusing incidents. I was coming upstairs, from deck to cabin.

Superbly dressed mulatto at the landing: "Got a cabin check, sir?" showing me one.

"No; I have not."

"Can't come up."

"But I paid cabin fare."

"Can't come up."

Here a white official, who knew me, interfered and apologized.

San Francisco at last! We all went in a body ashore. The cabmen thought here was a prize of greenhorn mountaineers. They came round us in swarms. "Lick House?"—"American Exchange?" — "Cosmopolitan?" — "Who wants a hack?" was screamed into our ears. The young men screamed back, "What Cheer House! Russ House! Occidental! This way, gentlemen!" etc. They soon saw that they had better let us alone. We mounted, and dashed off to the Oakland wharf. Not open yet; what shall we do? We shall ride about town. Pomroy and myself rode to the Lick House, where he wished to get a bundle, which he had left in Cobb's room. He dismounted at the ladies' entrance, and I sat on horseback and held his horse.

As he opened the door, the porter said, "What do you want?"

"Never mind," and he ran upstairs.

Porter came out and said to me, "What does that man want?"

"Mr. Cobb," said I.

Door shuts. Presently out he comes again. "Who is that man?"

I gave him no answer.

Again: "Where did that man come from?"

I took no notice of him. Door shuts again, and I could see through the glass that he went upstairs to look after that man. After a little,

Pomroy came and told me that the porter had finally recognized him, and apologized.

Our glorious party is, alas, dissolving. Three—Cobb, Bolton, and Linderman—left us here; the rest of us now rode down again to the wharf, and found the gate open. Went in and tied our horses. Went across the way and again took a cup of coffee, and ate heartily of doughnuts. Back to the waiting room and dozed. At 11:30 got on board the boat for Oakland. Landed at the pier, we galloped alongside the swift-moving cars, the young men hurrahing. The race was kept up pretty evenly for a litle while, but soon the old steam horse left us behind, and screamed back at us a note of defiance. We went on, however, at a sweeping gallop, through the streets of Oakland, saluted only by barking dogs; dismounted at the stable, bid each other good-night, and then to our several homes; and our party, our joyous, glorious party, is no more!

Alas, how transitory is all earthly joy! Our party is but a type of all earthly life; its elements gathered and organized for a brief space, full of enjoyment and adventure, but swiftly hastening to be again dissolved and returned to the common fund from which it was drawn. But its memory still lives; its spirit is immortal.

BIBLIOGRAPHICAL NOTES

EARLIER EDITIONS

1. A JOURNAL OF RAMBLINGS THROUGH THE HIGH SIERRAS OF CALIFORNIA BY THE "UNIVERSITY EXCURSION PARTY"
Francis & Valentine, Commercial Printing House, 517 Clay Street, San Francisco. 1875. 103 pages; illustrated with 9 photographic prints. Size of page, 8½ x 5¼ inches. Bound in blue cloth.

The illustrations are of the following subjects: (1) Great Yosemite Fall [with the ten members of the party in the foreground]; (2) The Grizzly Giant; (3) The High Sierras, from Glacier Point; (4) The Gates of the Valley, from Inspiration Point [showing workers constructing the wagon-road]; (5) Bridal Veil Fall; (6) The Heart of the Sierras—Lake Tenaya; (7) Day-dawn in Yosemite—The Merced River; (8) North Dome—South (Half) Dome [with Linderman, Cobb, and Bolton mounted]; (9) Montgomery St., San Francisco—Where Our Trip Ended.

[It has been stated that only twenty-five copies were printed, but it is almost certain that there were more than that number, although the exact quantity is not known. Professor J. N. LeConte is under the impression that 12 copies were made for each member of the party.]

2. RAMBLINGS THROUGH THE HIGH SIERRA. By Joseph LeConte. In *Sierra Club Bulletin*, Volume III, No. 1, San Francisco, January, 1900; pages 1-107.

12 illustrations (halftones), of which 11 are from photographs of scenery by J. N. LeConte and 1 is a reproduction of the frontispiece of the 1875 edition.

Journal of Ramblings

[This number of the *Sierra Club Bulletin* has long been out of print and is extremely scarce.]

3. RAMBLINGS THROUGH THE HIGH SIERRA. By Joseph LeConte. [Seal of the Sierra Club.] Publication No. 21 of the Sierra Club, San Francisco. 1900.

[This is a reprint from the *Sierra Club Bulletin*, without changes, excepting the paper cover which bears the above title. It is not known how many copies were printed, but the number was not large. Those remaining on hand in 1906 were destroyed in the San Francisco fire.]

4. ROUGH NOTES OF A YOSEMITE CAMPING TRIP. By Joseph LeConte. In *Overland Monthly*, New Series, Volume VI, San Francisco, October, November, December 1885; pages 414, 493, 624.

[Contains part of the material of the *Ramblings*.]

5. A JOURNAL OF RAMBLINGS THROUGH THE HIGH SIERRA OF CALIFORNIA BY THE UNIVERSITY EXCURSION PARTY. By Joseph LeConte. San Francisco: The Sierra Club, 1930.

[1500 copies were printed by Taylor & Taylor, San Francisco, December 1930. Five illustrations were included. The edition was edited by Francis P. Farquhar.]

6. RAMBLINGS THROUGH THE HIGH SIERRA. By Joseph LeConte. Sierra Club, 1950 [*in* Volume III of the offset reprint of Volumes I-V of the *Sierra Club Bulletin*, a 500-copy edition, bound in buckram, printed in New York by New York Lithographing Corporation, in which the 12 plates (see item 3, above) are reproduced in 7 pages of a separate signature of illustrations within Volume III].

7. A JOURNAL OF RAMBLINGS THROUGH THE HIGH SIERRAS OF CALIFORNIA. By Joseph LeConte. Sierra Club, 1960.

[2500 copies were printed by the New York Lithographing Corporation, September 1960, with minor changes in pagination of the preliminaries and restoration of all the original illustrations.]

8. [The present version is a paperback reprint of the above edition with changes in pagination and the omission of two photographs.]